Man is a transitional being; he is not final.

The step from man to superman is the next approaching achievement in the earth's evolution.

It is inevitable because it is at once the intention of the inner Spirit and the logic of Nature's process.

—*Sri Aurobindo*

ON THE WAY TO SUPERMANHOOD

OTHER BOOKS BY SATPREM

Mother, a biography in 3 volumes:
1. *The Divine Materialism* (1980)
2. *The New Species* (1983)
3. *The Mutation of Death* (forthcoming)

The Mind of the Cells, essay (1982)

*Sri Aurobindo or
the Adventure of Consciousness,* essay (1984)

MOTHER'S AGENDA
1951-1973
13 volumes

Recorded by Satprem in the course of countless private conversations with Mother, the daily log of her fabulous exploration in the cellular consciousness of the body. Twenty-three years of experiences which parallel some of the most recent theories of modern physics. The key to man's transition to the next species. *(Volumes 1, 2, 3, 12 & 13 published)*

Satprem

ON THE WAY

to

SUPERMANHOOD

translated from the French by
Luc Venet

INSTITUTE FOR EVOLUTIONARY RESEARCH
200 Park Avenue, New York

For information address:
  in the U.S.:
  Institute for Evolutionary Research
  200 Park Avenue, Suite 303 East
  New York, New York 10166

  in India
  Mira Aditi Centre
  Aspiration Auroville
  Kottakuppam 605104
  Tamil Nadu

Library of Congress Cataloging in Publication Data

Satprem, 1923—
  On the way to supermanhood.

  Translation of: La genèse du surhomme
  Bibliography: p.
  1. Spiritual life. I. Title
BL624.S2613 1986   110   85-23187
ISBN 0-938710-11-7

Manufactured in the United States of America
Cover design by Charles Peale

Contents

At the feet of Truth

Or we may find
when all the rest has failed
Hid in ourselves
the key of perfect change[1]

−Sri Aurobindo

THE SECRETS are simple. Because Truth is simple. It is the simplest thing in the world − that is why we do not see it. There is but *one* Thing in the world, not two, as the modern physicists and mathematicians have begun to realize, and as a child well knows as he smiles at the waves on a sun-swept beach where the same foam seems to have rolled in since the beginning of time, recalling a great rhythm that wells up out of ancient memory and weaves days and sorrows into a single story, so old it feels like an unchanging presence, so encompassing in its immensity it even embraces the glides of a sea gull. And everything is contained in one second, the sum of all ages and all souls, all within one simple little point glistening for an instant on the wild foam. But we have lost that point, and that smile, and the singing second. So we have tried to restore that Oneness by addition: $1 + 1 + 1$ . . . like our computers, as if adding up all possible knowledge from every conceivable direction would finally yield the right note, the one note that brings forth song and moves the worlds and the heart of a forgotten child. We have tried to manufacture that Simplicity for every pocketbook, but the more we multiplied our clever push buttons, to simplify life, the farther away the bird flew, and the smile – even the sparkling foam is polluted by our equations. We are not even entirely sure our body is still ours – the beautiful Machine has devoured everything.

Yet that one Thing is also the one and only Power, because what shines in one point shines also in all other points. Once that is understood, all the rest is understood; there is but one Power in the world, not two. Even a child knows that: he is king, he is invulnerable. But the child grows up; he forgets. And men have grown up, and nations and civilizations, each in its own way seeking the Great Secret, the simple secret – through war and conquest, through meditation or magic, through beauty, religion or science. Though, in truth, we do not know who is most advanced: the Acropolis builder, the Theban magician, the Cape Kennedy astronaut, or the Cistercian monk, for one has rejected life in order to understand it, one has embraced it without understanding it, another has left a trace of beauty, and still another, a white trail in a changeless sky – we are merely the last on the list, that's all. And we still have not found our magic. The point, the potent little point, is still there on the open beach of the world; it shines for whoever will seize it, just as it shone before we were humans under the stars.

Others, however, have touched the Secret. Perhaps the Greeks knew it, and the Egyptians, and certainly the Indian Rishis of Vedic times. But secrets are like flowers on a beautiful tree; they have their season, their unseen growth and sudden blossoming. There is a "time" for everything, for the conjunction of stars above our heads and the passage of the cormorant over the foam-flecked rock, and perhaps even for that foam itself, cast up for an instant from the swell of the wave; everything moves according to a single rite. And so do men. A secret, that is, a knowledge and power, has its own organic time; one little cell more evolved than others cannot embody the power of its knowledge, that is, change the world, hasten the blossoming of the great tree, unless the rest of the evolutionary terrain is ready.

But the time has come.

It has come, it is bursting out all over the earth, even if the unseen flower still looks like a festering boil: students behead Gandhi's statue in Calcutta, the old gods crumble, minds fed on intellect and philosophy cry for destruction and invite the outland Barbarians to help them break their own prison, just as the ancient Romans did; others call for chemical paradises – any way is better than this one! And the earth gasps and groans through all its cracks, its countless cracks, through all the cells of its great body in transformation. The so-called evil of our time is a new birth in disguise, which we do not know how to handle. We are before a new evolutionary crisis as radical as must have been the first human aberration among the great apes.

But since the terrestrial body is one, the remedy is one, like Truth, and a single point transmuted will transmute all the others. That point, however, is not to be found in the improvement of our laws, our systems or sciences, our religions, schools of thought or many-hued isms – all those are part of the old Machinery; not a single nut needs to be tightened, added or improved anywhere: we are suffocating in the extreme. Moreover, that point has nothing to do with our intelligence – that is what has contrived the whole Machine in the first place – or even with improving Man, which would amount only to glorifying his weaknesses and past greatness. "The imperfection of Man is not the last word of Nature," said Sri Aurobindo, "but his perfection too is not the last peak of the Spirit." Indeed, this point lies in a future beyond the grasp of our intelligence, but it is growing in the depths of the being like the flowers of the flame tree when all its leaves have fallen.

But there is a handle to the future, provided we go to the heart of *the* thing. But where is that heart if it is not in what we deem beautiful and right and good according to our human standards? One day, the first reptiles out of the water sought to fly, the first primates out of the jungle cast a strange new look over the world: one and the same irresistible urge was making them contemplate another state. And perhaps all the transforming power was already contained in that simple look TOWARD something else, as if that look, that urge, that point of the unknown crying out, had the power to unlock the floodgates of the future.

Indeed, that point contains all, is all-powerful; it is a spark of the innumerably unique solar Self, which shines in the heart of every man and thing, in each point of space, each second of time, each fleck of foam, ceaselessly becoming the ever more it has glimpsed in a fraction of a second.

The future belongs to those who give themselves unreservedly to the future.

And we assert that there exists a future far more marvelous than all the electronic paradises of the mind: man is not the end, any more than the archeopteryx was, at the height of the reptiles — how could anything possibly be the culmination of the great evolutionary wave? We see it clearly in ourselves: We seem to invent ever more marvelous machines, ceaselessly expand the limits of the human, even progress towards Jupiter and Venus. But that is only a seeming, increasingly deceptive and oppressive, and we do not expand anything: we merely send to the other end of the cosmos a pitiful little being who does not even know how to take care of his own kind, or whether his caves harbor a dragon or a mewling baby. We do not progress; we inordinately inflate an enormous mental balloon, which may well explode in our face. We have not improved man; we have merely colossalized him. And it could not have been otherwise. The fault does not lie in some deficiency of our virtues or intellectual capacities, for pushed to their extreme these could only generate supersaints or supermachines — monsters. A saintly reptile in its hole would no more make an evolutionary summit than a saintly monk would. Or else, let us forget everything. The truth is, the summit of man — or the summit of anything at all — does not lie in perfecting to a higher degree the type under consideration; it lies in a "something else" that is not of the same type and that he aspires to become. Such is the evolutionary law. Man is not the end; man is a "transitional being," said Sri Aurobindo long ago. He is heading toward supermanhood as inevitably as the minutest twig of the highest branch of the mango tree is contained in its seed. Hence, our sole true occupation, our sole problem, the sole question ever to be solved from age to age, the one that is now tearing our great earthly ship apart limb from painful limb is how to make this transition.

Nietzsche said it also. But his superman was only a colossalization of man; we saw what he did as he trampled over Europe. That was not an evolutionary progress, only a return to the old barbarism of the blond or brunet brute of human egoism. We do not need a super-man, but something else, which is already murmuring in the heart of man and is as different from man as Bach's cantatas are from the first grunts of the hominid. And, truly, Bach's cantatas sound poor when our inner ear begins to open up to the harmonies of the future.

It is this opening, this new development we would like to investigate in the light of what we have learned from

Sri Aurobindo and Her who continued his work, the
modus operandi of the transition, so we can grasp the
handle ourselves and work methodically at our own
evolution—perform experimental evolution—the way
others try to make test-tube embryos, though they may
only hear the echo of their own monsters.

The secret of life is not in life, nor that of man in man,
any more than the "secret of the lotus is in the mud from
which it grows," said Sri Aurobindo; and yet the mud and
a ray of sun combine to create a higher degree of harmony. It is this site of convergence, this point of transmutation, that we must find. Then, perhaps, we will
rediscover what a quiet child on a beach contemplated in
a fleck of wild foam, and the supreme music that spins
the worlds, and the one Marvel that was awaiting its
hour.

And what seemed to be humanly impossible will become child's play.

1

The Mental Fortress

OUR DIFFICULTIES always stem from the belief that we alone remedy them. As long as our intellectual power (or inadequacy) does not play a role and our greater or lesser capacities are not actively involved, we feel that our endeavor is doomed to failure. Such is the deep-seated belief of mental man. We know its results all too well. But even if they *were* flawless within their own scope, they would still conceal a supreme flaw, which is to bring in only what is contained in our own intelligence or muscles—except when life or happenstance frustrates our plans. In other words, our mental existence is a closed system. Nothing gets into it but what we ourselves put in. This is the cornerstone of the Great Fortress. Its second inevitable trait is the mechanical rigor of its process: everything runs in a closed circuit according to the thought, plan, or muscle we set in motion, since nothing can come into the process except what we have concocted. And everything is measurable down to the least dyne, centidyne and millidyne we have expended: we get exactly what we bargained for—but that was already anticipated in the intelligence quotient put into play. That is, the system is perfectly and hermetically sealed down to the last cranny. There is not a single crack, except, once again, when life happens to upset more or less opportunely our faultless measures. The third inevitable trait stemming from the other two is its impeccable thoroughness: nothing escapes its attention, and what does will soon be worked out, put into equation and "programed" to be fed back into the machine and further inflate the great expanding balloon. Everything is, of course, perfectly objective, since we all wear the same glasses; even our instruments scrupulously behave according to the results we want them to show. In short, the system operates rigorously and flawlessly according to specification. Like the sorcerer of old, we have traced a mental circle on the ground, stepped into it, and here we are.

But that just may prove to be a stupendous illusion.

In fact, the illusion is being shattered despite ourselves. What we take to be a dreadful disarray is a great array of new energies coming to pump fresh air into our lungs of mentalized earthlings. "New energies" . . . there is a phrase with a mystical ring to it which would undoubtedly draw dark frowns from the materialist. But let us admit it (before circumstances force us to do so with our nose to the ground), today's materialists are as outdated as yesterday's religionists; they are in a closed, stifling, predictable and obsolete system. Both are products of the mental circle, the obverse and reverse of the same coin, which is proving counterfeit. The real point lies not in god versus no-god, but in something else: the point is to step out of the circle and see how one breathes on the other side—one breathes very well on the other side, so well, in fact, that it is like breathing for the very first time ever.

Thus, we shall not effect the passage with our own strength; if such were the condition, no one could do it, except spiritual athletes. But those athletes, filled with meditations and concentrations and asceticism, do not get out either, although they may seem to. They inflate their own spiritual ego (a kind worse than the other one, far more deceptive, because it is garbed in a grain of truth) and their illuminations are simply the luminous discharges of their own accumulated cloud. The logic of it is simple: one does not get out of the circle by the power of the circle, any more than the lotus rises above the mud by the power of the mud. A little bit of sun is needed. And because the ascetics and saints and founders of religions throughout the ages only reached the rarefied realms of the mental bubble, they created one church or another that amazingly resembled the closed system from which they originated, namely, a dogma, a set of rules, the Tables of the Law, a one and only prophet born in the blessed year 000, around whom revolved the beautiful story, forever fixed in the year 000, like the electrons around the nucleus, the stars around the Great Bear, and man around his navel. Or, if they did get out, it was only in spirit, leaving the earth and bodies to their habitual decay. Granted, each new hub was wiser, more luminous, worthy and virtuous than the preceding one, and it did help men, but it changed nothing in the mental circle, as we have seen, for thousands of years — because its light was only the other side of one and the same shadow, the white of the black, the good of evil, the virtue of a frightful misery that grips us all in the depths of our caves.

This implacable duality which assails the whole life of mental man — a life that is only the life of death — is obviously insoluble at the level of the Duality. One might as well fight the right hand with the left. Yet, that is exactly what the human mind has done, without much success, at all levels of its existence, offsetting its heaven with hell, matter with spirit, individualism with collectivism, or any other isms that proliferate in this sorry system. But one does not get out by the decree of any ism pushed to its perfection: deprived of its heaven, our earth is a poor whirling machine; deprived of its matter, our heaven is a pale nebula filled with the silent medusas of the disembodied spirit; deprived of the individual, our societies are dreadful anthills; and deprived even of his "sins," the individual loses a focus of tension that helped him to grow. The fact is, no idea, however lofty it may seem, has the power to undo the Artifice—for the very good reason that the Artifice has its value and season. But it has also its season, like the winged seed tumbling over the prairies, until the day it finds its propitious ground and bursts open.

Indeed, we shall not get out through an idea but through an organic Fact.

Nature has always shown us that she knows perfectly well what she is doing. We think ourselves superior to her because we mentalize her, pigeonhole her, and have harnessed some of her secrets, but in so doing we are still under her law. If she was indeed able to evolve the iridescent tentacles of the actinia out of a pale protoplasm, so it could better seize its prey, and offer to our gaze this multicolored panorama of millions of different earthly species, we must believe that she had also good reasons to differentiate her human actinias, each seizing the prey he could in the polychromatic network of his thousands of thoughts, feelings and impulses. If this mental circle, this very dismaying hydra, has closed in upon our species, it is certainly not a useless trap, over which we could have jumped had we been smarter. So why make it in the first place if it were only to get out of it? If the visionary shepherd of Upanishadic times could have jumped directly to supermanhood, then what is the evolutionary sense of all this sweat and blood? Nothing is useless in this world. We have yet to find the pain that does not have its secret power of growth.

But its use is not as the mind imagines in the arrogance of its knowledge and discoveries, for the mind always mistakes the instrument for the Master. We thought that the mental tool was both end and means, and that that end was an increasing, ever more triumphant and rigorous mastery over the mental field, which it has colonized with marvelous cities and less marvelous suburbs. But that is only a secondary end, a turbulent by-product, and it turns out that the major effect of the Mind in man has not been to make him more intelligent (intelligent with respect to what? The mouse in its hole has the perfect intelligence for its own terrain), but to individualize him within his own species and endow him with the power to change—while the other species were invariable and only individualized as a general type—and finally to make him capable of casting a look at what exceeds his own condition. With this individualization and power of variation began the "errors" of man, his "sins," his afflicting dualities; yet his capacity for error is also a secret capacity for progress, which is why all our moralities based on right or wrong and all our flawless heavens have failed and will forever fail—if we were flawless and irreproachable, we would be a stagnant and infallible species, like the shellfish or the opossum. In other words, the Mind is an instrument of accelerated evolution, an "evolver." In fifty years of scientific development, man has progressed more than during all the prescientific milleniums. But progress in what sense? To be sure, not in the sense of the fallacious mastery, nor in the quality of life or the degree of comfort, but in the sense of the mental saturation of the species. One cannot leave a circle unless one has individually and collectively exhausted the circle. One cannot step alone onto the other side; either everybody does it (or is capable of doing it) or nobody does it; the whole species goes together, because there is but one human Body. Instead of a handful of initiates scattered among a semianimal and ignorant human mass, the entire species is now undergoing its initiation or, in evolutionary terms, its supreme variation. We have not passed through the mental circle for the sake of sending rockets to the moon, but in order to be individually, innumerably and voluntarily capable of effecting the passage to the next higher circle. The breaking of the circle is the great organic Fact of our times. All the dualities and opposite poles, the sins of virtue and the virtues of sin, all this dazzling chaos were the instruments of the Work, the "tensors," we could say, bending us to the breaking point against a wall of iron — which is a wall of illusion. But the illusion falls only when one decides to see it.

That is where we are. The illusion is not dead; it even rages with unprecedented violence, equipped with all the arms we have so obligingly polished up for it. But these are the last convulsions of a colossus with feet of clay — which is actually a gnome, an oversized, overoutfitted gnome. The ancient sages of India knew it well. They divided human evolution into four concentric circles: that of the men of knowledge (Brahmins), who lived at the beginning of humanity, in the "age of truth"; that of the nobles and warriors (Kshatriya), when only "three fourths of the truth" was left; that of the merchants and middle class (Vaishya), who had only "half of the truth"; and finally ours, the age of the "little men," the Shudra, the servants (of the machine, of the ego, of desire), the great proletariat of regimented liberties — the "Dark Age," Kali Yuga, when no truth is left at all. But because this circle is the most extreme, because all the truths have been tried and exhausted, and all possible roads explored, we are nearing the right solution, the true solution, the emergence of a new age of truth, the "supramental age" Sri Aurobindo spoke of, like the buttercup breaking its last envelope to free its golden fruit. If the parallel holds true between the collective body and our human body, we could say that the center governing the age of the sages was located at the level of the forehead, while that of the age of the nobles was at the level of the heart, that of the age of the merchants, at the stomach, and the one governing our age is at the level of sex and matter. The descent is complete. But that descent has a meaning – a meaning *for matter*. Had we stayed forever at the forehead level of the divine truths of the mind, this earth and body would never have been changed, and we would have probably ended up escaping into some spiritual heaven or nirvana. Now, everything must be transformed, even the body and matter, since we are right in it. Ironically, this is the greatest service this dark, materialistic and scientific age may have rendered us: to compel such a plunge of the spirit into matter that it had either to lose itself in it or to be transformed with it. Absolute darkness is but the shadow of a greater Sun, which digs its abysses in order to raise up a more stable beauty, founded on the purified base of our earthly subconscious and seated erect in truth down to the very cells of our bodies.

O Force-compelled, Fate-driven earth-born race,
O petty adventurers in an infinite world
And prisoners of a dwarf humanity,
How long will you tread the circling tracks of mind
Around your little self and petty things? ...
A Seer, a strong Creator, is within,
The immaculate Grandeur broods upon your days,
Almighty powers are shut in Nature's cells. [2]

This impossible endeavor (for us) is not impossible for the Great Executrix who has led the evolutionary play to this crucial turning point. It is She who can. We just have to seize her secret springs, or rather, let Her seize hold of us and collaborate in our own evolution by having an intimate understanding of the Great Process. None of the spiritual virtues and athletics of the old closed system will be of any use. What is needed is a sort of radical leap, fully conscious and with eyes wide open, a very childlike surrender to the gods of the future, an iron resolve to track the momentous Illusion down to the smallest recesses, a supreme opening to the supreme Possibility— which will lift us up in Her arms and carry us upon Her sunlit road even before we are satisfied of having taken a quarter of a step toward Her. For indeed "there are moments when the Spirit moves among men . . ., there are others when it retires and men are left to act in the strength or the weakness of their own egoism. The first are periods when even a little effort produces great results and changes destiny."[3]

We are just at that moment.

2

The Great Process

THE SECRET of a circle is in the very next circle, as the secret of the arrow is in the goal it pursues, and if we could retrace our steps to the Master Archer, we would have the secret of secrets, the central point that determines this circle and all circles, the goal of all goals. But the pursuit is said to be a long one, and we must go back one step at a time, from the tool to the Hand that guides the tool, since we ourselves started out by being that tool: a little vital antenna groping around a self of life before discovering itself as a moth or a millipede, a little mental antenna quivering inexplicably around a nimble self before discovering itself as a man among men, and that other, still undefined antenna which seems to dispense with senses and thought to take us toward another, still greater self. Until the day we arrive at the great Self and shall be fulfilled. We will have found the Master of all tools and the full meaning of the journey.

But how could we possibly know the secret of that which now seems an undefined and disturbing nonself, possibly even destructive of what we so concretely know as self, we who are at the end of this mental circle, in this age of the servants of the ego and ambiguous enjoyments of a little thinking self? . . . Actually, the path is made by walking it, as in a forest. There is no path, it does not exist: it has to be made. And once we have walked a few feet, apparently in the dark, we will realize that our groping steps led to a first clearing, and that we were all the while guided, even in our darkest stumblings, by an infallible Hand that has already directed our millipede meanderings. For, in fact, the goal we pursue is already within; it is an eternal Goal. It is a Future that is millions of years old and as young as a newborn child. It is opening its eyes to everything, constantly staring in wonderment. To find It is to enter constant wonder, a new birth of the world at each instant.

But at least we have signposts to help us take these first steps, and if we pose questions about man's future (not pose questions in the sense of a theoretician spinning his vain web and adding one idea to another only to inflate the same old story, but in the sense of a sailor plotting his course, because there is a channel to go through even as the sea crashes against the reefs), we will perhaps discover a few clues by studying the old animal circle, when we were still only the future of the ape.

An animal is simple. It is wholly contained in its claws, its prey, its senses, in the northerly wind that raises the imperceptible scent of rain and the image of a deer in the tall grass. And when it is not in motion, it is perfectly still, without a quiver of doubt about the past or anticipation of the future. It does exactly what is needed, at the moment it is needed. And as for the rest, it is in harmony with the universal rhythm. But when the first great apes began to emerge from their forests, something had already changed. They cast a less direct look at the world: the past already had a weight and the future its worries—they were engaged in the first act of introspection, which we know well, with its burden of pain and error. What seemed such a futile and vain exercise in terms of simian efficiency has become the cornerstone of our towering mental edifice; everything, even Einstein, was contained in that simple and totally superfluous exercise. And at the edge of another forest, made of concrete and titanium, we may be standing before an identical, even more stupendous mystery, and no less superfluous, as we stop for a second amid the rush of things, this time not to reflect but to cast a mute look, as if blinded, at this thinking and speculating and suffering and struggling first person. We thus raise a strange new antenna, quite meaningless and seemingly pointing at nothing, yet it holds the secret of the next cycle, and marvels next to which the splendid twentieth-century rockets are like clumsy children's toys. We are engaged in the introspection of the second kind; we are knocking at the door of the unknown of the third circle, holding the thread of the Great Process.

The secrets are simple, as we have said. Unfortunately the mind has seized this one, as it seizes everything, and has pressed it into the service of its mental, vital or spiritual ego. It has discovered certain powers of meditation or concentration, more refined energies, higher mental planes that were like the divine source of our existence, lights that were not from the moon or stars, more direct and almost superhuman faculties — it has climbed the ladder of consciousness — but all that only served to sublimate and rarefy a rare human elite; sublimate it so much, in fact, that there did not seem to be any other issue to this climb than an ultimate leap out of the dualities and into the changeless peace of eternal truths. A few souls were "saved," possibly, while the earth went on its dark course, increasingly dark. And what should have been the earth's secret became heaven's. The most frightful schism of all time was accomplished, the bleakest duality was imprinted on the heart of the earth. And the very ones who should have been humankind's supreme unifiers became its dividers, the Founding Fathers of atheism, materialism and all the other isms that struggle for our world. The earth, duped, had no other recourse but to believe exclusively in herself and her own strength.

But the damage does not stop there. Nothing is stickier than falsehood. It sticks to the soles of our shoes even though we have turned away from the wrong path. Others had indeed seen the earthly relevance of the Great Process—the Zen Buddhists, the Tantric initiates, the Sufis and others—and, more and more, disconcerted minds are turning to it and to themselves: never have so many more or less esoteric schools flourished. But the old error is holding fast (to tell the truth, we don't know whether "error" is ever an appropriate term, for the so-called error always turns out to be a roundabout route of the same Truth leading to a wider view of itself). It took so much effort out of the Sages of those days, and out of the lesser sages of these days, so many indispensable conditions of peace, austerity, silence and purity for them to achieve their more or less illumined goal, that our sub-conscious mind was as if branded by a red-hot iron with the idea that, without special conditions and special masters and somewhat special mystical or innate gifts, it was not really possible to set out on that path, or at best the results would be meager and proportionate to the effort expended. And it was still, of course, an individual undertaking, a lofty extension of book learning. But this new dichotomy threatens to be more serious than the other one, more potentially harmful, between an unredeemed mass and an "enlightened" elite juggling lights about which anything can be said since there is no microscope to check it. Drugs, too, are a cheap ticket to dizzying glimpses of dazzling lights. But we still do not have the key, the simple key. Yet the Great Process is there, the simple process. One has to admit to a major flaw in the method, and first, to a flaw in the goal pursued. What do we know of the goal, really, sunk in matter as we are, blinded by the onrush of the world? Our first immediate reaction is to cry, "It can't be here! It's not here! Not in this mud, this evil, this whirlwind, not in this dark and burdened world!" We must get out at all costs, free ourselves from this weight of flesh and struggle and from that surreptitious erosion in which we seem to be eaten up by thousands of voracious trivialities. So we have proclaimed the Goal to be up above, in a heaven of liberated thoughts, a heaven of art and poetry and music – any heaven at all is better than this darkness! We came here merely to earn the leisure for our own private heaven, bookish, religious, pictorial or aesthetic – the long vacation of the Spirit free at last. So we have climbed and climbed, poeticized, intellectualized, evangelized; we have rid ourselves of all that might weigh us down, erected a protective wall around our eremite contemplations, our cloistered yoga, our private meditations, traced the white circle of the Spirit, like new spiritual witch doctors. Then we stepped into it, and here we are.

But, in so doing, we are perhaps making as great a mistake as that of the apprentice human in his first lake dwelling who would have claimed that the Goal, the mental heaven he was gropingly discovering, was not in the commonplaceness of daily life, in those tools to carve, those mouths to feed, those entangling nets, those countless snares, but in some ice cave or Australasian desert – and who would have discarded his tools. Einstein's equations would never have seen the light of day. By losing his tools, man loses his goal; by discarding all the grossness and evil and darkness and burden of life, we may go dozing off into the blissful (?) reaches of the Spirit, but we are completely outside the Goal, because the Goal might very well be right here, in this grossness and darkness and evil and burden—which are gross and dark and burdensome only because we look at them erroneously, as the apprentice human looked erroneously at his tools, unable to see how his tying that stone to that club was already tying the invisible train of our thought to the movement of Jupiter and Venus, and how the mental heaven actually teems everywhere here, in all our gestures and superfluous acts, just as our next "heaven" teems under our eyes, concealed only by our false spiritual look, imprisoned in the white circle of a so-called Spirit which is but our human approximation for the next stage of evolution. "Life . . . Life alone is the field of our Yoga," exclaimed Sri Aurobindo. [4]

Yet the process, the Great Process, is here, just as it began as long ago as the Pleistocene era—that idle little second, that introspection of the second kind—but the movement revealed to the monkey and the movement revealed to the spiritualist of ages past (and surpassed) are in no way an indication of the next direction it is to take. There is no continuity—that is a delusion! There is no refinement of the same movement, no improving upon the ape or man, no perfecting of the stone tool or the mental tool, no climbing higher peaks, no thinking loftier thoughts, no deeper meditations or discoveries that would be a glorification of the existing state, a sublimation of the old flesh, a sublime halo around the old beast—there is SOMETHING ELSE, something radically different, a new threshold to cross, as different from ours as the threshold of plant life was from the animal, another discovery of the already-here, which will change our world as drastically as the human look changed the world of the caterpillar–yet it is the same world, but seen with two different looks–another Spirit, we might say, as different from the religious or intellectual spirit or the great naked Spirit on the heights of the Absolute, as man's thought is different from the first quivering of a wild rose under a ray of sunlight–yet it is the same eternal Spirit but in a greater concretization of itself, for, in fact, the Spirit's true direction is not from the bottom up, but from the top down, and it becomes ever more in matter, because it is the world's very Matter, wrested bit by bit from our false caterpillar look and false human look and false spiritual look–or, let us say, recognized little by little by our growing true look. This new threshold of vision depends first on a pause in our regular mental and visual routine–and that is the Great Process, the movement of introspection of the second kind–but the path is entirely new: this is a new life on earth, another discovery to make; and the less weighed down we are by past wisdom, past ascents, past illuminations, all the disciplines and virtues and old gilded frills of the "Spirit," the freer we are and more open to the new, the more the path shall spring up under our feet, as if by magic, as if it sprang from that total desecration.

This superman, whom we have said is the next goal of evolution, will therefore in no way be a paroxysm of man, a gilded hypertrophy of the mental capacity, nor will he be a spiritual paroxysm, a sort of demigod appearing in a halo of light and outfitted with an oversized consciousness (cosmic, of course) streaked with bolts of lightning, marvelous phenomena and "Experiences" that would make the poor laggards of evolution pale with envy. It is true that both things are possible, both exist. There *are* marvelous Experiences; there *are* superhuman capacities that would make the man in the street turn pale. It is not a myth; it is a fact. But Truth, as always, is simple. The difficulty does not lie in discovering the new path; it lies in clearing away what blocks the view. The path is new, completely new; it has never been seen before by human eyes, never been trodden before by the athletes of the Spirit, yet it is walked every day by millions of ordinary men unaware of the treasure at hand.

We will not theorize about what this superman is. We do not wish to think him; we wish to become him, if possible, keeping away from the old walls and old lights, remaining as completely open as possible, as alert to the great process of Nature as possible — just walking, for that is the only way to do it, *solvitur ambulando*. Even if we don't get very far, who knows, we may still emerge in a first clearing that will fill our hearts, souls and bodies with sunlight, for everything is one and everything is saved together or nothing is.

Then others will come who will move on to a second clearing.

3

The Sunlit Path

THERE ARE two paths, Sri Aurobindo used to say, the path of effort and the sunlit path. The path of effort is well known. It is the one that has presided over our entire mental life, because we try to reach for something we do not have or think we do not have. We are full of wants, of painful holes, of voids to be filled. But the void never gets filled. No sooner is it filled that another one opens up, drawing us into yet another pursuit. We are like an absence of something that can never find its presence, except in rare flashes, which vanish immediately and seem to leave an even greater void. We may say that we lack this or that, but we really lack one thing, and that is self: There is an absence of self. For what is really self is full, since it *is*. Everything else comes and goes, but is not. How could what *is* ever be in need of anything else? An animal is perfectly in its animal self, and once its immediate needs are satisfied, it is in equilibrium, in harmony with the universe. Mental man is not in his self, though he believes he is—he even believes in the greatness of his self, because it must have size, like everything else, and there must be bigger and lesser selves, more or less voracious or talented or saintly or successful selves; but by doing so, man avows his own weakness, because how could what is self be more or less self? It is, or it is not. Mental man is not in his self: he is in his inventory, like a mole or a squirrel.

But then, *where* is that elusive self? ... To ask the question is to knock at the door of the next circle, to engage in the movement of introspection of the second kind. And here, too, it is pointless to theorize on the nature of the self; it must be sought and discovered experientially. Now, we did say that the method had to take place in life and matter, because we can very well shut ourselves up in a room, keep out the sounds of the world, keep out its desires, tensions and countless tentacles; we can hold all these things at arm's length and, maybe, from within our little inner circle catch a glimpse of self, some ineffable transcendence, but the minute we open the door of our room and let go of our grip, everything will fall back on us again, like a mantle of seaweed over a diver, and we will find ourselves exactly as before, only less capable of putting up with the noise and swarm of little cravings awaiting their hour. It is not by the grip of our virtues or exceptional meditations that we shall clear away that mantle, but by something else and in another way. For, indeed, the self we have to find is not a superself; it is something else altogether. We will therefore start with what we are and as we are, at the physical level of everyday life.

We are Bill Smith, a name without a meaning, a legal artifice to tie us to the great Machine and to an obscure genealogy we do not know much about, except that we are the son of our father, who was the son of his father, who was the son of his father, and that evidently we shall be the father of our son, who will be the father of his son, who will be the father of his son, and so on endlessly. And we walk up and down the great boulevard of the world, here or there, in a Los Angeles which looks more and more like Tokyo, which looks more and more like Mexico City, which looks more and more like every city in the world, just as one anthill looks like another. We can very well take a plane, but we will find ourselves again everywhere. We are French or American, but, to tell the truth, that is only history and passports, another artifice to bind us hand and foot to one machine or another, while our brother in Calcutta or Rangoon walks the same boulevard with the same question, under a yellow, red or orange flag. All this is the vestige of the hunting grounds, but there is not much left to hunt, save ourselves, and we are well on our way to being crushed out of that possibility, too, under the steamroller of the great Machine. So we go up and down the stairs, make phone calls, rush around, rush to vacation or enjoy life, like our brother under a yellow or a brown skin: in English, French and Chinese, we are harassed on all sides, exhausted, and we are not quite sure whether we are enjoying life or life is enjoying us. But it goes on and on all the same. And through it all, there is something that goes up and down, rushes and rushes, and sometimes, for a second, there is a sort of little cry inside: "Who am I? Who am I? Where is me? Where am I?"

That brief second, so vain and futile amid this gigantic haste, is the real key to the discovery, an all-powerful lever that seems like nothing – but truth seems like nothing, naturally, for if it seemed like something, we would already have wrung its neck, to pigeonhole it and harness it to another piece of machinery. It is light; it slips through the fingers. It is a passing breeze that refreshes all.

Then the question sinks a little deeper. In fact, it is not that it sinks or intensifies; it is as if a first breath of air enabled us to appreciate better the daily suffocation we live in and revealed deeper layers to our eyes, other, subtler coverings. We are indeed Bill Smith, a legal and national artifice, a little mechanized cog that would like to get out of the machine. But what is behind Bill Smith? There is a man walking a boulevard, going up and down the great mental roller coaster, humming with a thousand thoughts, of which none truly matters, none remedies his sorrow or desire; there is what the latest book thinks, what that billboard or those headlines scream, what the professor or schoolmaster or friend or colleague or neighbor said — a thousand passersby milling in the inner street — but where is the one who does not pass, the lodger of the dwelling? There is yesterday's experience, which ties in with the accident of the day before, which ties in with . . . a gigantic telephone network, with switches, relays and instant communications, but which really communicates nothing, except the same rehashed and self-contained story, which keeps swelling up and swelling up and curling back onto itself and unrolling a sum of past that never makes a true present, or a future that is but the sum of a million acts adding up to zero — where is *the* act, where? Where is the self of that addition, the minute of being that is not the result of the past, the pure touch of sunlight that escapes that machinery, even more merciless than the other one? There is what our fathers and mothers have put into us, and books, priests, partisans, grandfather's cancer, great-uncle's lust, the good of this one, the less good of that one; there are the Tables of the Law of iron, the thou-cannots, thou-should-nots, Newton and the churches, Mendel and the law of gestation of germ cells — but what germinates in all that? Where is *the* Germ, the pure unexpected seed suddenly bursting open, the **Thou-Can** like a stroke of grace in this implacable round conditioned by the fathers of our fathers inside the mental fortress? There is this little man walking along a boulevard, going up and down the same avenue a thousand times; inside, outside, it's all the same, like nothing walking in nothing, anybody inside anything, John or Peter with only different neckties: between this lamppost and that one nothing has *happened*. There was nothing, not a single second of being!

But, suddenly, on this boulevard, there is a sort of second-degree suffocation. We stop and stare. What do we stare at? We don't know, but we stare. All of a sudden we are no longer in the machine; we are no longer in it, we never were! We are no longer Bill Smith or American or New Yorker, the son of our father or the father of our son, our thought, or heart or feelings, or yesterday or tomorrow, or male or female or anything of the kind — we are something else altogether. We don't know what, but it stares. We are like a window opening.

Then it vanishes; the machine takes over again.

But, alone in our room that night, if we go over the day, review the thousand gestures and steps and faces, the coming and going in that whirling grayness in which nothing seems to have happened, a day among a thousand others that are like a deserted semidarkness, we suddenly notice a little spark of light rising to the surface, oh, so tiny, so fleeting that it is almost like a passing firefly, and it is that lone little second when we stopped in the midst of the frenzy, that little second of nothing, that useless misstep, that faltering of thought, that snag of being — that's all that remains of the day, the only existing second, the only inhabited moment. That's all that *was* among a million empty seconds.

From then on, the suffocation becomes very effective. It is as if our being had begun to feel an imperceptible fissure in the dark, some crack we do not even know lets light in — and what light, since it seems even darker than before? But we come back to it despite ourselves. There is like another air circulating, an impalpable change of density, and at the same time like a fire being lit, an obscure black fire which knows nothing except that it needs, needs, needs something else so very much.

Out, out with the mind and its candle flares,
Light, light the suns that never die![5]

So Bill Smith—who is no longer anything really, who is less and less something, who escapes through all the pores of his skin—stops again, stops more and more often in the midst of the great bustle, and he does not even ask a question anymore, he does not even expect an answer: he has become *the* question, a living fire of nothing, a pure, pounding question, a growing absence, so poignant it is almost like a presence. He stops here, stops there, raises unseeing eyes to this street poster, that man dressed in brown, those millions of shadowy humans; he is no longer even a thought, not even a feeling: he is one step removed from himself, from the something that stirs, goes up and down, relays thoughts and feelings and memories and desires, and runs like a well-oiled clock—wound up since when?—unwinding and unwinding, inside, outside, it is all the same. He is that site of sudden stillness, that cry of suffocation, that blind stare of a newborn from a world yet to be, it seems, but which beats as the only existing thing in this nonexistence. He is in a no-man's land of being, at times a tearing state of nonself, so tearing it seems that tear is the only measure of being in him.

Now the waste-land, now the silence
A blank dark wall, and behind it heaven. [6]

So at night, alone in his room, he looks again at those brief seconds that shine inexplicably, that even radiate as though projecting beyond themselves, suffusing everything they touch with drops of their light; the man in brown, the absurd poster, the ray of sun on a park bench are as if imbued with special life, captured, photographed down to the least detail – they live, they *are*. All the rest is like dust swallowed up into a limbo of nonexistence. Yet there was no thinking in him, no feeling, no memory, not even any I, especially not any I; it was the one second when all that was gone, when he had stumbled upon a rather dizzying non-I.

Then the vain walker discovers something else. He notices that those scattered little drops of light (is it light? it is rather like a sudden eruption into something else, a vibration so swift it escapes our habitual perceptions and colorful translations; it vibrates, it is something vibrating, like a note of another music for which we have no ear yet, colored brush strokes of another country for which we have no eyes yet), those points of another intensity, those tiny little landmarks of a blind geography, are indestructible, as it were. They live and go on living long after they have passed by, as if they never passed away. And indeed they never pass away; they are the only thing that does not pass. It seems as if that little tear there, in front of that poster or park bench, that sudden stare before nothing, maintains its own intensity; that drop of something else, that sudden little cry for nothing, goes on being, as if it had settled into a secret cleft in us and kept on vibrating and vibrating, one drop added to another without ever dissipating, without ever being lost; and it keeps building up and building up like an unfailing reservoir in us, a haven in the making, a set of batteries gradually being charged with another intensity, and which is like a beginning of being.

We begin to set out upon the sunlit path.

We are no longer quite in the machine, although it may still snag us from time to time, but only to make us feel its crushing tension, its dark rotation in a nothing which connects with nothing which connects with nothing—we have felt another air, even if it seems like nothing, and we can no longer put up with this nonexistence, which rambles from one end of the planet to the other, from one phone call to another, one appointment to another, which goes up and down the endless grind where nothing ever happens, except the same sempiternal story with different faces and different names and different words, on this boulevard or another—it has to *be*! Between this lamppost and that one, this third floor and the fourth, this 9 a.m. and 9:30 a.m. of a clock that times nothing, something has to *be*, to *live*, this footstep has to have its eternal meaning as if it were unique in the millions of hours on the dial, this gesture has to be borne by someone, this newspaper stand we pass, this rip in the carpet, this doorbell we ring, this second—*this* second—has to have its own unique and irreplaceable wholeness of existence as if it alone were to shine till the end of time—oh, not this nothingness walking in nothingness! Let it be, be, be! . . . We want to remember, remember all the time, and not just drift down the boulevard like a jellyfish. But remember what? We don't even know what has to be remembered—to be sure, not I or the machine, or anything that again connects one thing to another. A pure recall, which ends up becoming like a call, a fire burning for nothing, a little vibration of being that accompanies us everywhere and permeates everything, fills everything, each step, each gesture, each second, and which even extends behind us, as if we moved within another space, with that little fellow in the foreground who keeps going on, but who is no longer totally in it, who has already absconded, filled his lungs with another air, who hearkens to another song, runs to another rhythm—and it is almost like an eternal rhythm, very vast and soft. And all of a sudden, he raises his head in the middle of that boulevard; he pokes his head above the frenzy; and it is such a clear look, so luminous, almost joyful, sparkling, wide and sunny, taking everything in at a glance, so triumphant and sure and crystalline—instant royalty. We are! *It* is!

We are on the sunlit path, as if carried by that growing little vibration of being.

We had no need of silence, of a well-insulated room, of keeping life's tentacles at a distance. On the contrary, the tighter they grasp and try to suffocate us, the more deafened we are by all that racket of life, and the more it burns inside, the hotter it is, the greater the need to be that and only that, that other vibrating thing without which we cannot live or breathe—forgetting it even for a second is to fall into total suffocation. We are treading the sunlit path amidst the world's darkness—inside, outside, it's all the same, alone or in a crowd we are forever safe, nothing and nobody can take that away from us! We carry our secret royalty everywhere we go, moving ahead gropingly within another geography, which gradually reveals secret harbors and unexpected fjords and continents of peace and glimpses of unknown seas reverberating with the echo of a vaster life. There is no more wanting or not wanting in us, no more compulsion to acquire this or that, no struggle to live or become or know: we are borne by another rhythm that has its spontaneous knowledge, its clear life, its unforeseeable will and lightning effectiveness. A different kingdom begins to open up to us; we cast another look at the world, still a little blind and unknowing, but insightful, as if pregnant with a reality yet unborn, made wide by a knowledge still unformulated, a still shy wonderment. Perhaps we are like that brother ape of not so long ago who looked at his forest with a strange look, at his mates who ran and climbed and hunted so well but were not aware of the clear little vibration, the odd marvel, the sudden stillness that seemed to sunder the dark clouds and stretch far, far away, into a vastness vibrating with creative possibilities.

4

The Fork in the Road

FROM THIS point on, the road forks, and taking one path rather than the other entails far-reaching consequences that can extend over an entire lifetime. Not that one path is true and the other false, for we tend to believe that everything is ultimately true, since it exists, but this is a truth that grows, and falsehood is merely dawdling or persisting in a truth that has outlived its time and usefulness. From the moment we have broken loose from the machine, the outer as well as the inner one (the former is really a reflection or expression of the latter, and once we change inside, we will necessarily change outside; if we cease to "mentalize" life, it will cease being a mental round and become another life), from that moment on, we literally begin to have a certain "latitude." No longer bound to the shadowy little person like a tethered goat, we can choose to move in two distinct directions. We can take the ascending path, that is, subtilize ourselves more and more, cast off the earthly burden, soar off in the enchanted little rocket of light we are beginning to sense, and come upon freer realms of consciousness, explore airy ranges, discover higher mental planes that are like the pure source of everything that takes place, distorted and approximate here, the angel face of what is looking more and more like a caricature.[7] It is very tempting, so tempting in fact that all the sages and rather hasty seekers, or even simply those we would today call advanced minds or geniuses, have taken it—it has lasted for thousands of years. But, unfortunately, once we reach those higher strata, it is very difficult to come back down; and even if we wish to come down, moved by some charitable or humanitarian urge, we notice that the ways above are fairly ineffective here. There seems to be an unbridgeable gulf between that light and this darkness, and what we want (or are able) to bring down from up there reaches here diminished, diluted, disfigured, leaden, finally to be lost in the Machine's great morasses.

> *But too bright were our heavens, too far away,*
> *Too frail their ethereal stuff;*
> *Too splendid and sudden our light could not stay;*
> *The roots were not deep enough.*[8]

It is the age-old story of the ideal versus "reality." The ideal is inevitably realized, since it is but an advanced future, but it is a long-drawn-out course in which the truth often appears thwarted, slighted. Therefore, it is this course, the faulty transmission between the "summits" and the plains, which ought to be shortened.

But perhaps the "summit" is not located up above. Perhaps it is everywhere here, at ground level, simply covered up by the Machine and all our successive evolutionary layers, like the diamond in its matrix. If the path of ascent is the only way out, then we all had better get out once and for all. And if the saint really is the triumph of the ape, one may doubt that evolution will ever reach its satisfying, and blessed, goal, and that the entire earth will become hallowed. What then of the others, those

who balk at saintliness? We do not believe that evolution's ultimate design is a moralistic sorting out of the
elect and the damned. Evolution is not moralistic; it just
is, and it grows its entire tree so all its flowers can produce blossoms. Evolution is not ascetic; it embraces
everything sumptuously and opulently. Evolution has not
deserted the earth, or it would never have started on
earth. Nature is not incoherent; she is wiser than our
mental coherence, wiser even than our saintliness.

But she is slow. That is her shortcoming.

So we want to shorten the course. We want to com-
press evolution, effect a concentrated evolution, while
still respecting its methods. And since Nature embraces
everything, we shall follow her example. Since she does
not run away from herself but strives always to develop
her seeds into fruits, we shall endeavor to bring that seed
to fruition, to make what is already inside, and around
and everywhere, blossom. Only, we have to find that particular seed. There are many wild seeds in this world —
although they, too, have their charm and usefulness.
Thus, we shall not seek our summit up above but all the
way down at the bottom, for our secret may already be
there, in the simple, infallible Truth that one day cast
this seed upon our good earth. Then we will perhaps
discover that what we were looking for is so near that
there is no distance to travel, no unbridgeable gulf, no
faulty transmission or dilution of power across ranges of
consciousness, and that the Truth is right here, immediate and all-powerful, in each atom, each cell, each
second of time.

In short, the method will not be arrowlike, spurning all
hindrances in order to soar to spiritual heights, but all-
embracing; it will not be a precipitous ascent but a descent or, rather, an unveiling of the Truth which pervades
everything, down to the very cells of our body.

5

The New Consciousness

THERE IS a radically new fact. It is not old. It goes back only a few years. It is a new beginning on earth, and perhaps in the universe, as simple and bewildering as must have been the appearance of the first mental vibration among the great apes. A new beginning is not aware of itself, not thunderous or earthshaking. It is simple and hesitant, frail as a young sapling, and one does not quite know whether it is still yesterday's wind that one feels or some new breath, almost the same and yet so different, which leaves one a little stunned and incredulous, like a marvel caught unawares, a smile ensnared, which vanishes instantly if one looks a little too long. A beginning is a thousand tiny beginning strokes that come and go; brush by and scurry off; crop up from nowhere, without rhyme or reason, because they are of another law; laugh and make fun of everything, because they are of another logic; reappear when we thought them lost and leave us looking foolish when we thought we had seized them, because they are of another rhythm or, perhaps, another way of being. And yet, yet these tiny little lines gradually make up another picture; these repeated little strokes make a nameless something that vibrates differently and changes us unnoticeably, plucking a chord that does not quite know its note but ends up creating another music. Everything is the same, and everything is different. One is born without realizing it.

Therefore, we cannot say precisely how it works, any more than the apes of old could say what had to be done to control thought. We can, however, try to describe some of these elusive little strokes, indicate a general direction and, along with our traveler of the new world, follow step by step the thread of a discovery that seems at times incoherent but eventually makes a coherent whole. We have never been in that country before. It even seems to take shape under our feet, almost to grow by our look, as if noticing this curve, that almost mischievous gleam, encouraged it to grow and draw this dotted line under our feet, this other curve, and that enchanting hill, toward which we run with a pounding heart. Our traveler of the new world is first and foremost an observer: nothing escapes his attention, not one detail, not the slightest encounter, the least conjunction or hardly noticeable correspondence – the marvel is born in droplets, as though the secret were of an infinitesimal order. He is a microscopic observer. For maybe there are no "big" things or small ones, but one and the same supreme flowing whose every point is as supremely filled with consciousness and meaning as the sum total of all universes, as if, really, the entire goal were at each instant.

Hence we have filled each and every wasteland of our day – there is no more waste – we have infused the vacancy between two acts with being, and even our acts are no longer so completely caught up in the Machine. We can talk, make phone calls, write or meet people, but behind, in the background, something continues to be, vibrating,

vibrating very softly, like a breath from a far-off sea, the flowing of a little river in the distance; and if we stop for a moment in mid-gesture and take but a single step back, we are instantly in that ever so fresh little river, that open space, that easy expanse, and we sink into it as into the repose of Truth, because only Truth is at rest, since it is. Everything else stirs, comes and goes, and changes. Strangely enough, this sort of slippage or shifting of the center of being does not loosen our grip on life, does not throw us into a sort of dream state we would be tempted to call hollow. On the contrary, we are utterly awake—it even looks as if the sleeper were in the one who talks, writes and telephones—in a state of alertness, but not alert to the machine's wheelworks, the play of the features, the calculation of the next step, the whirl of appearances: we are engrossed in something else, as if listening behind our head, in that vibrating expanse, that leisurely flowing; and sometimes we feel variations of intensity, changes of rhythm, sudden pressures, as if a finger of light were pressing there, bringing something to our notice, calling our attention to a particular point by shining its light. Then, without knowing why, we utter some words, make a gesture, or, on the contrary, are kept from making a gesture, we turn here instead of there, smile when the person we were talking to seemed so unpleasant, or, on the contrary, dismiss him rapidly when he seemed so well intentioned. And everything is exactly as it should be, to a T. What we did or said was exactly what had to be done or said, just where we had to turn to avoid the accident or have the necessary encounter—two days or two hours later, in utter amazement, we understand the meaning or exactness of our action. It is as if we had been introduced to a functioning of truth.

And we begin to be struck by a first peculiarity. These indications coming to us, these perceptions or sudden pressures, have nothing in common whatsoever with those coming from above when pursuing the path of ascent: they are not revelations, not inspirations or visions or illuminations, not the flashes and thunder of the higher planes of the mind. They seem, rather, to be a very humble and material functioning, one concerned with the tiniest detail, the slightest passing breath, this street corner, that automatic gesture, these thousand little comings and goings. It looks almost like a functioning at ground level.

But at the beginning this functioning is still unsure. We are constantly snatched back by the old machinery, the habit of mulling over thoughts, judging, deducing, calculating, and immediately it is as if a veil fell, a screen came between the quiet clarity behind and the arduous whirlwind here: communications are jammed. Again we have to take a step back and find the comfortable expanse—and it is irritating, uncommunicative and apparently indifferent to our fate, opposing a neutral silence, an unrelieved blankness to the question we send it and which would yet call for an immediate answer. So we yield once more; we start up the machine again—only to realize that everything was blank behind so we would not move in front, and that the time for an answer had not yet come. We keep stumbling along and persisting, trustful but awkward outwardly (or in front), when circumstances would call for swiftness and efficiency, and those who work with the old reason may scoff, as perhaps the old veteran anthropoid scoffed at the clumsiness of the apprentice man: we miss the branch. We fall and pick ourselves up. We go on. But gradually, as our "demechanization" gains ground, grows sure-footed and more perfect, the communications become clearer, the perceptions more accurate and precise. We begin to unravel a whole jumbled network that had previously seemed like logic itself. From within the tranquil clarity, we notice a multitude of movements rising from below, from outside, from others; it is a mixture of vibrations, a cacophony of minuscule impulses, a battlefield, an arena filled with obscure contenders, blind drives, dark flashes, microscopic and stubborn wills. And all of a sudden, in all that muddle falls a tiny little drop from our quiet river—without our wanting it or trying or even asking for it—and everything loosens up, smooths out, disappears, dissolves. That face there in front of us, this grating little circumstance, that knot of difficulty, this stubborn resistance vanishes, melts away, smooths out, opens up as if by magic. We begin to enter mastery.

But it is a curious sort of mastery—it does not obey us at all! On the contrary, the minute we try to use it, it eludes us completely, slips through our fingers, pokes fun at us and leaves us looking foolish, like an apprentice sculptor trying to imitate the stroke of the Master: our stroke misses. We even hit our fingers. And we learn. Perhaps we learn not to want anything. But it is a little more complicated than that—complicated from our standpoint, of course, because everything is complicated on this side; it is complexity itself. In fact, it is simple. We are learning the law of rhythm. Because Truth is a rhythm.

It has swift flowings, precipitous cascades, slack stretches that go deep into themselves like a sea into a deeper sea, like a great bird into the infinite blue. It has sudden urgings, minute diamond points that probe and pierce, expansive white silences like a steppe in the eternity of ages, like a fathomless gaze spanning lives upon lives, oceans of sorrow and toil, continents of struggle, road upon road of prayer and fervor. It has abrupt bursts, miraculous instantaneous outcomes, a long, untiring patience that follows each step, each gesture, each quiver of being like a murmur of eternity upholding the minute.

And behind that instant or swordlike flash, that vast slowness unfolding its trail of infinity, that burning point bursting out, that commanding word or compelling pressure, there always lies a kind of tranquil clarity, a crystalline distance, a little snow-white note that seems to have traveled and traveled across expanses of calm light, filtered down from an infinity of clear-sighted softness, trickled from a vast sun-washed prairie where no one suffers, acts or becomes—a sweeping expanse upholding the little note, the gesture, the word, and the abruptness of an act springing from a fathomless peace where the noise of time and the press of men and the swirl of sorrows are cloaked in their mantle of eternity, already healed, already past, already wept over. For Truth enfolds the world as in a great robe of softness, in an infinite sky where our black birds and birds of paradise, sorrows from here and there, gray wings and pink ones melt away. All becomes one, adjusts to that note, and is in tune; all is simple and stainless, without trace, imprint or doubt, because all flows from that music, and this minute immediate gesture harmonizes with a great swell that will still roll in long after we have left.

But if "I" interferes, even for a second, a little eddy, a little me, a sticky and hard little nodule, a little self-will, everything goes awry and starts grating, wants or does not want, hesitates and fumbles—there is instantaneous muddle: the consequence of the act, the consequence of everything, the haunting memory, the sticky trace, the toil in everything. For it is not enough to be clear in our head; we have to be clear everywhere.

In that tranquil clarity behind, we stumble in fact upon a second level of confusion, a deeper one (this is truly a descending path). As our mental machinery grows quieter, we appreciate the extent to which it covered everything up–all existence, the least gesture, the slightest flutter of an eyelash, the tiniest vibration, like a voracious and ever-growing hydra–and we see the bizarre fauna it concealed starting to appear in broad daylight. This is no longer an arena but a teeming swamp seething with all sorts of psychological microbes: a throng of minuscule reflexes like the jerks of the pseudopod, semiautomatic reactions and erratic impulses, thousands of desires, complete with the larger speckled fish of our instinctive idiosyncracies, our innate tastes and distastes, our "natural" affinities and the whole discordant play of our sympathies and antipathies, attractions and repulsions–a mechanism that goes back to the Precambrian era, a massive residue of the habit of devouring one another, a huge multifarious vortex in which selective affinities are scarcely more than an extension of gustatory affinities. Thus, there is not only a mental machinery but also a vital one. We desire and we want. Unfortunately, we want all sorts of contradictory things, which mix with our neighbor's contradictory wills, forming a blind mixture; and we do not even know if the triumph of today's little will is not preparing tomorrow's downfall, or whether this satisfied desire, this austere and righteous virtue, that noble taste, that well-intentioned "altruism" or stern ideal is not working some disaster worse than the evil we were trying to cure. All this vital hodgepodge, adorned with mental labels and justifications, which philosophizes and spouts its wonderful and faultless reasons, now appears in its true colors, we could say, in the quiet little clearing where we have taken our position. And here, too, we gradually apply the same process of "demechanization." Instead of rushing headlong into our sensations and emotions, our tastes and distastes, our certainties and uncertainties, like the animal into its claws (but without its deftness), we take a step back, we pause and let the torrent abate, we rein in the reflex, the peremptory judgment, the mixed or less mixed emotion – at any rate, it is a mixture for the clear little stream flowing in the background, the undeceivable ray of sunlight: suddenly the rhythm is broken, the water no longer clear, the ray fragmented. These breaks, these interferences, these jarring intrusions become more and more unbearable. It is like a sudden lack of oxygen, a sinking into mud, an intolerable blindness, the shattering of a little song behind, which made life smooth and vast and rhythmical, like a great prairie wafted by a breeze from elsewhere.

For there is really a rhythm of truth behind, and around and everywhere, a vast and tranquil flowing, a space of weightless time in which the days and hours and years seem to follow the unalterable movement of the stars and moons, rising and falling like a tide from the depths of time, harmonizing with the movement of the whole, and filling this present little fleeting second with an eternity of being.

That is where we have taken our position, in that little clearing. It is our base, our crystal-clear retreat, our Himalaya of the boulevards, our tiny unalterable song. And finally we realize there is no need "to do" or "not to do," to get involved or not, to want or not, to master; all we need is to be there, securely, and to let that little rhythm flow into things, that clear cadence into the darkness of circumstances, that tranquil ray onto all beings. And everything straightens out, simply, marvelously, without our knowing why, by the single fact of *being* there. All the shadows are dissolved, order is restored, peace and harmony are settled, the rhythms are corrected – for there is no real evil, no enemy or contradictions, only discordant rhythms. When we are in harmony with ourselves, everything is in harmony – but not according to our ideas of good and evil, happy and unhappy, failure and success, but according to another order, which gradually turns out to be infallible and endowed with extended foresight–an order of truth.

And each minute becomes clear. Each face behind its shadows, each circumstance behind its turmoil, each chance step, each accident, each fall reveals its meaning, like a core of pure truth trying to become. There is no more judging, no more wrong impulses, no haste or tension or eagerness, no fear of losing or missing, no disquieting uncertainties or soon questioned certainties: there is *that*, which flows, which is true, and which only wants to be truer and truer, because Truth is life's great sweetness, peace and breadth of being, exactness of each gesture and perfection of each moment.

We have entered a new consciousness, a consciousness of truth.

And again we are struck by the same phenomenon. This is not a sublime consciousness like that found on the peaks of the Spirit, which is only a paroxysm of self. There is no sparkling here, but minuscule sparks that crowd our seconds with a sweetness of eternity; no dazzling ranges, just little clearings where breathing is easy every instant; no cosmic visions, but tiny little drops of truth that seem to fill each point with total meaning; no prophecies or predictions; no ecstasies, no revelations, just a simple and clear look that does what is needed when it is needed and humbly prepares the marvels to come; no momentous revolutions, but a little revolution every moment hinging on an imperceptible sun in the heart of things; no big things, no little ones: a sameness of truth growing with each step and each gesture–one could almost say a consciousness of the Truth of Matter.

This is the great new Fact in the world. This is the new consciousness announced by Sri Aurobindo, the microscopic beginning of an earth-of-truth. Because they had not seen it (or the time had not come), the sages of old searched for heaven by scaling the high peaks of the Spirit. But heaven is in our midst. It is growing by our look, becoming stronger with each obstacle, each gesture of truth, each second really lived; it is outlining its graceful hills under our surprised footsteps and vibrates imperceptibly in a little eruption of being wrested from our great wastelands.

6

The Breaking of the Limits

WE HAD set out in search of a self amid all this inner and outer machinery; we so much needed something other than this genetic sum, this legal fiction, this *curriculum vitae* which is like a curriculum of death, this sum of actions and daily gestures adding up to zero or perpetually in hope of an inscrutable and elusive something, this crest of existence forever slipping away from under our feet and receding into the distance, toward another wave, the more or less happy repetition of the same old story, of the same "program" stored in the computer with our parents' chromosomes, our studies, our formative and deformative years; something that was not the attaché case we lug around everywhere, nor the stethoscope, nor the pen, not the sum of our feelings nor the sum of our changeless thoughts, nor the total of a thousand faces and appointments that leave us forever the same and alone in our little island of self which is not self, which is millions of things crammed into us from the outside, from around and above and below us, from life, from the world, from other beings—where is the self? What is me in all that? Where am I? The question had become so unbearable that one day we stepped outside—

stepped into nothing, which was perhaps something, but it was everything, the only way out of the leaden island. Then, little by little, in the tiny empty interval between this shadow of mechanical self and that something, or nothing, which watches it all, we saw a flame of need grow in us, a need that became more and more intense and burning as the darkness grew thicker in and around us, an inexplicable flame leaping in that stifling nothingness. And slowly, very slowly, like a vague dawn emerging from under the night, like a faraway city wrapped in fog, we saw twinkling little lights start to appear, faint signs, so faint they looked like lights floating on a dark sea, which could have been ten feet or ten miles away, unless they were the reflection of stars or the phosphorescence of noctilucas beneath the waves. But even that nothing was already something in a world filled with such unsurpassed nothingness. So we persevered. The little flame of need settled in us (or was it outside us, or in our stead?); it became our companion, our presence amid an absence of everything, our gauge, our ever-burning intimacy. And the more it grew, calling out from within us, calling so desperately in this empty and suffocating nothing, the brighter the signs grew, twinkled a little everywhere beneath our steps, as if to say, "See? See?," as if calling the new world brought it to birth, as if something answered. Soon, the fragile little lights were tied to one another, became steadier, formed into lines, coordinates, channels, and we began to enter another country, another consciousness, another way of being— but where is "me" in all this, the one who directs and owns, that singular traveler, the center that is neither of the ape nor of man?

So we looked intently right and left: where is "me," who is "me"? . . . There is no me! Not a trace, not a single ripple of it. What is the use? There is this little shadow in front, which appropriated and piled up feelings, thoughts, powers, plans, like a beggar afraid of being robbed, afraid of destitution; it hoarded desperately on its island, yet kept dying of thirst, a perpetual thirst in the middle of the lovely sheet of water; it kept building lines of defense and fortresses against that overwhelming vastness. But we left the leaden island; we let the stronghold fall, which was not so strong as all that. We entered another current that seemed inexhaustible, a treasure giving itself unsparingly: why should we hold back anything from the present minute when at the next one there were yet other riches? Why should we think or plan anything when life organized itself according to another plan, which foiled all the old plans and, sometimes, for a second, in a sort of ripple of laughter, let us catch a glimpse of an unexpected marvel, a sudden freedom, a complete disengagement from the old program, a light and unfettered little law that opened all doors, toppled the ineluctable consequences and all the old iron laws with the flick of a finger, and left us stunned for a minute, on the threshold of an inconceivable expanse of sunlight, as though we had stepped into another solar system – which is perhaps not a system at all – as if breaking the mechanical limits inside had caused the same breaking of the mechanical limits outside. Maybe because the Machinery we are facing is one and the same: The world of man is what he thinks it; its laws are the result of his own constraint.

Yet this other way of being is not without logic, and that logic is what we should try to capture, if possible, if we want to pass consciously into the other state, not only in our inner life but in our outer one as well. We must know the rules of the passage.

To tell the truth, they do not reveal themselves easily – because they are too simple. It takes tireless experimenting, looking, observing, and above all – above all – looking at the microscopic. We imagine that the great primates of the past that were uncertainly progressing toward manhood must have discovered the secret of the other state gradually, in thousands of little split seconds, when they noticed that the mysterious little vibration that came between them and their mechanical act had the power to make their gesture and the result of their gesture different: a nonmaterial principle was surreptitiously starting to change matter and the laws of tree climbing. And, we further imagine, they were perhaps eventually struck by the insignificance of the movement that triggered such formidable consequences (which is why it escaped them for so long; it was too simple): "It" never concerned itself with big things, the great affairs of apes, but with minuscule gestures, the chance pebble one picks up on the edge of the path and holds a moment in one's palm, the ray of sun playing on one young sapling among millions of other identical but vain saplings in the forest. But that sapling and that pebble are looked at differently. And everything is in that difference.

Therefore, nothing is too small for the seeker of the new world; the slightest fluctuation of the inner vibratory state is carefully noted, along with the gesture that accompanies it, the circumstance that springs up or the face that passes. But we did say "vibration": thoughts have very little to do with this; they belong to the old mental acrobatics and are about as consequential for the new consciousness as tree climbing was for the first thought. It is more like a change of inner coloration, a play of fleeting shadows and sudden sunshine, of lightness and heaviness, a minute alteration of the rhythm – sharp jolts or leisurely flowings, abrupt pressures that compel our attention, sudden breaks in the clouds, moments of malaise, inexplicable sinkings.

Nothing is useless; there are no vain saplings in the forest, no nuisances, nothing to discard, no unhappy circumstances, no adverse locations, no untimely encounters, no unfortunate accidents – everything is good for the seeker of the new world, everything is his field of study. ... It almost seems as though everything were *given* to him so he could learn the trade. Thus, the seeker begins to put his finger on the first rule of the passage: Everything is part of it. Everything points in that direction! There is no nuisance, no foes, no obstacles, no accidents, no negative things – everything is supremely positive, gives us signs, invites us to the discovery. There are no insignificant things, only moments of unconsciousness. There are no contrary circumstances, only wrong attitudes.

But, then, what is the attitude that brings the new consciousness, the look that makes a difference? The attitude is simple, we have said: one must first have severed all ties with the machine and live in the expanse behind. We say "behind," but to tell the truth we do not know whether there is front, back, top or bottom; it is only a distance from "ourselves," the old shadow, a sort of position both above and behind, as if that shadow were only part of a picture among many other things we looked at – but *who* does the looking, where is the Self that looks? ... It is indeed a strange self, which is not myself. It feels as if "myself" were no longer inside the body, hanging in the center of the mental and vital spider web, but as if the body were inside myself, along with many other things. And as the disconnection from the machinery grows more absolute, this self seems even to extend outward, to touch many other points, apparently capable of living in many different places, without any concern for distance, as if it no longer depended on the sense organs and could, perhaps, live innumerably, here or there, depending on where the beam is focused. . . . It is an innumerable self.

The basic condition seems therefore to establish that clear little expanse "behind," that increasing flow: the medium must be clear, otherwise everything is distorted and there is no look at all, only the same old hodgepodge. But that clarity is only a basic condition *for* something else: the instrument is being cleaned to be used. And we come back to our question: What sort of look will "unearth" the new consciousness? . . . For it is indeed a matter of "unearthing": it is here, not millions of miles away in the heavens or in space. It is so close that we do not see it; it seems so much like nothing that we walk right past it, as the ape walked past the river a thousand times without noticing the torrent of energy that could change its world.

Our look is false because it perceives everything through the distorting prism of its routine, which is multifarious and subtle, made of thousands of years of habits which are as distorting in their deviltry as they are in their wisdom. This is the residue of the anthropoid, which had to erect barriers to protect his little life, his little family, his little clan, draw a line here, a line there, boundary markers, and generally insure his precarious existence by encasing it in a shell of individual and collective self. It follows that there is good and evil, right and wrong, useful and harmful, dos and don'ts—we have slowly become entangled in a huge police network in which we scarcely have the spiritual freedom to breathe—and even that air is polluted by countless decalogues that are barely one step above the pollution by the carbon monoxide of our engines. In short, we are forever "correcting" the world. But we are beginning to realize that this correction is not all that straight. Never for a moment do we stop putting our multicolored glasses on things in order to see them in the blue of our hopes, the red of our desires, the yellow of our morals and ready-made laws, and in black, in the endless grayness of a machinery that keeps grinding and grinding forever. The look – the true look – that will have the power to break free from this mental spell is therefore the one that will be able to cast itself on things clearly, without immediately "correcting" them: to rest here, upon this face, that circumstance or object the way one gazes at the infinite sea, without trying to know or understand – especially not to understand, because that is again the old machinery trying to solidify something – to let itself be carried by that tranquil and fluid infinity, to bathe in what we see, to sink into the thing, until slowly, as if from far away, from the depths of a tranquil sea, there emerges a perception of the thing seen, of the puzzling circumstance or face near us; a perception that is not a thought, not a judgment, hardly a sensation, but is like the true vibratory content of the thing, its special mode of being, its quality of being, its innermost music, its relation with the great Rhythm that flows everywhere. Then, slowly, the seeker of the new world will see a sort of little spark of pure truth in the heart of the object, circumstance, face or accident, a little cry of true being, a true vibration beneath all the black and yellow and blue and red coatings – something that is the truth of each thing, each being, each circumstance, each accident, as if the truth were everywhere, every instant, every step, only coated in black. The seeker will thus have put his finger on the second rule of the passage and the greatest of all the simple secrets: Look at the truth that is everywhere.

Armed with these two rules, firmly established in his sunlit position, that quiet clearing, the seeker of the new world moves within a greater self, perhaps infinite, which

embraces this street and these beings and all the little
gestures of the hour; he moves steadily on, as though carried by a great rhythm, which also carries the beings
and things around him, the thousands of encounters
sprung from nowhere and disappearing into the distance;
he looks at this little walking shadow, which seems to
have walked so long, walked for many lives perhaps,
repeated the same small gestures, stumbled here and
there, exchanged the same comments on the mood of the
times; and it all seems so similar, so mixed with
sweetness that this street and these beings and passing
encounters seem to be cast from the same mold, issued
from the depths of night, recalled from the same identical
story, under the sky of Egypt or India or Vermont, today,
yesterday or five thousand years ago—and what has
really changed? There is this little being walking with his
fire of truth, his fire of need, so intense amid the turmoil
of time—a fire is perhaps the only thing that is truly *he*, a
call of being from the depths of time, an unchanging cry
amid the immense flow of things. And what is he calling
for, this being; what is he crying for? Is he not in that vast
and growing sunlight, in that rhythm carrying everything? He is and he is not. He has one foot in an un-
troubled eternity and the other stumbling and groping in
the dark—the other in a little self of fire yearning to fill
this second of time, this empty gesture, this step among
thousands of similar steps, with a fullness of true existence as complete as all the millenia put together, with as
unfailing an exactness as the crisscrossing of the stars
above our heads; yearning for everything to be true, true,
completely true and filled with meaning, in this enormous
whirlwind of vanity; yearning for this line he crosses, this
street he goes down, this hand he extends, this word he
utters to be linked to the great flowing of the worlds, to
the rhythm of the stars, to the lines, the countless

lines that furrow this universe and form a total song, a truth filled with the whole and each fragment of the whole. So he looks at all these little passing things, he fills them with his fire of entreaty, he looks and looks at that little truth everywhere as if it were going to burst out, forced into being by his fire.

And it is true that the world starts changing before our eyes and that nothing is insignificant anymore, nothing is separate from the rest. We witness a great, total birth. Our simple look has strange extensions, our little gesture a reverberating echo. But here again, it is a timid birth; it is more like scattered little hints of birth. The seeker stops and stares at a scattering of little outbreaks, of happenings with no apparent connection, a little like the ancient hominid staring at a pliant branch here and a vine and a piece of flint over there before tying them into a bow and felling his prey in full career. He does not know the connections – they almost have to be invented. But our inventions are only a discovery of what is already there, like the river and the vine in the forest. A new world is a discovery of new connections. Now, ours is the age of introspection of the second kind, when the invention, the true invention, is no longer one that will bring two material objects together by means of the subtle phenomenon of thought, but one that will be able to bring together that same matter and the subtler phenomenon of a second degree of consciousness, silent and without thought. The task of our age is no longer to perfect matter through matter, to enlarge matter by adding more matter to it – we are already suffocating under the monstrous plethora which fetters us and which, at bottom, is only an "improvement" of the ape's technique – but to transform matter through that subtler power, or rather, perhaps, to make it reveal its own innate power of truth.

*
* *

It is difficult to choose examples from those thousands of microscopic little experiences which one hardly knows whether to call experiences, coincidences or imaginations. Yet they keep cropping up, insisting, as if an invisible finger of light were guiding our steps, checking this gesture, exerting a subtle pressure on one point or another, until we understand – then the pressure is lifted and we move on to another point, which seems to come back again and again with the same obstinacy. An experience is a thousand experiences unaware of themselves. There is no recipe, no instruction sheet; the only way is to walk, stumble, walk more, until, all of a sudden, there is a little "ah!" which fills a thousand gaps at once.

There are two categories of "experiences," positive ones and negative ones, and they embrace everything from the little subjective entity that we are all the way to the great objective entity we move in. Then, at some point, this subjectivity and this objectivity melt, this little fragment of matter merges with the large one, and everything moves in a single movement. This is the breaking of the limits.

Among those innumerable beginning little bursts, the one that recurs most frequently is the interpenetration or interfusion of the inner and the outer, but in the opposite direction to that of materialistic mechanics. There, hitting our fingers results in a disorder in our inner substance; here, a disorder in our inner substance results in a blow in matter. This experience is repeated thousands of times, at every level of our being, so we clearly understand the process. It is negative at first, catching us in our weak spots, as if error were always the door to a greater truth. Thus, we have come out of our little clearing, once again snagged by the machine (one should say by pain, for it is truly a self of pain), and all the circumstances of life begin surreptitiously to change, sometimes even in a striking way which can go so far as a physical accident. Yet there was no evil thought, no old desire or restless agitation; there was only a little slipping into the old habit of being under a weight of anxiety, a darkening without apparent reason, a loss of the clear little ray. And everything starts grating, nothing accords, nothing meshes, every gesture is amiss, we twist an ankle on the stairway. We fall back into a sort of arduous effort, as if we were constantly pushing against a wall. So we stop for a moment, call back the silence, take one step back, rekindle that fire of need, which is really like a cry for air, and everything suddenly lightens, eases up, relaxes – the wall is gone. We have stepped back into the vastness, recaptured the rhythm, the little music in the depths of things; and all the circumstances start imperceptibly to turn in another direction, unexpected, light, casual, sprinkled with little smiles that flicker here and there, beckoning us. Sometimes, there is even a miraculous arrangement, but minuscule miracles that do not care to boast by displaying their power, that do not even want to be acknowledged, that only smile slightly if we point a finger at them, as if to say, "See how silly you are?"

Indeed, we feel quite silly. All of a sudden we step into an incredible landscape where little living lights seem to twinkle softly everywhere, winking gleefully, almost mischievously at us, as if doors were opening up on every side, drops of treasure were glistening like dew everywhere. All at once, everything seems to follow another law, to live according to another rhythm, as though our eyes had seen wrongly for centuries and now they are seeing correctly, the world becomes true, everything is revealed, everything is a revelation! We could almost say, "Let it be this way," for the circumstance to become exactly as we have seen it at that instant, to obey our command, to adhere inexplicably, as if there were perfect, instantaneous coincidence between matter and the look that opened up in us—everything is possible, everything becomes possible. It looks like a miracle, but it is not a miracle. There is no miracle, only connections we do not grasp. And the experience is repeated until we grasp it. It is fleeting, whimsical, and eludes us when we try to capture it; it depends on something else. And we come back again and again to that something else, which seems like nothing, which is simple as a smile, light as a breeze, yielding as a flower in the sun—maybe that is what total openness is, a kind of assent full of sunshine, to everything, at every second? But, first, there is always a blossoming inside, something that opens up and communicates instantly and directly with matter, as if the point of truth in us had joined and touched the same points of truth in matter. It all flows without breaks; what "it" wants here, in this point of "self," is also wanted there, in that point of matter, because it is one and the same substance, one and the same will, one and the same global self, one and the same rhythm. Fabulous horizons open up before us for a second, then disappear. The seeker has stumbled upon an elusive secret that holds the marvel of the new world in seed as certainly as the first thought of the ape held the seed of Einstein's marvels—but this is an unfettered marvel, completely free and independent of all external mechanisms, a kind of spontaneous springing out from within. He has put his finger on the third golden rule of the passage: From within outward. Life is no longer the result of a manipulation of external phenomena, an addition and combination of different kinds of matter by the power of the mental machinery, but the unfolding of an inner phenomenon that manipulates matter's truth by the inner truth—an unfolding of the truth in truth and by the truth.

And once again we are struck by the same phenomenon. These fleeting little bursts have nothing to do with "big things," the sensational and earthshaking affairs of men. They are humble miracles, one could say meticulous miracles of detail, as if the real key were there in the little stumbling everyday trifle caught by surprise, at ground level, as if, in fact, a victory won over a minute point of matter were more pregnant with consequences than all the trips to the moon and the huge revolutions of men – which in the end revolutionize nothing. This new functioning seems indeed to be radically new. It is unlike any of the so-called spiritual or occult powers one can obtain by scaling the ladder of consciousness: these are not prophetic powers, or healing powers, or powers of levitation – the thousand and one poor powers that have never healed the world's poverty – they are not dazzling lights that command men's attention for an instant, only to leave them afterwards as they were before, half asleep and afflicted with cancer; not brief, compelling impositions from above that come and upset the laws of matter, only to let it fall back the next moment into its heavy and stubborn obstinacy. It is a new consciousness – new, entirely new, like a young shoot on the tree of the world – a direct power from matter to matter, without interference from above, without descending course, distorting intermediary or diluting passage. Truth here answers truth there, instantly and automatically. It is a global consciousness, innumerably and infinitesimally conscious of the truth of each point, each thing, each being, each second. We could say a divine consciousness of matter, the very one that one day cast this seed upon our good earth, and these millions of wild seeds, and these millions of stars, which knows perfectly every moment all the degrees of its unfolding, down to the tiniest leaf – everything harmonizes when one harmonizes with the Law. Because, in fact, there is only one Law, a Law of Truth.

Truth is supreme effectiveness.

7

The Fire of the New World

BUT WHAT is this new consciousness that suddenly appeared in the year of grace 1969 of our evolution? (There may have been many other years of grace before, now buried under the rubble of the earth, and other human cycles that reached the point we have now reached and were destroyed perhaps for the very same reasons that threaten us today. Are we the topmost crest of the great evolutionary wave or simply the nth repetition of an attempt that has taken place many times before, here or in other universes?) This new consciousness may not be so new after all, but it became new for us and entered the field of practical realizations the very day we were able to establish a relation with it – we should perhaps say renew the relation with it, because since the beginning of time, here or on other earths, it may be eternally the same eternal Thing with which we establish different relations according to our degree of preparation. What seemed remote and divine to the orangutan is fairly close and far less divine to us, but the godheads of the future remain to be claimed, and there will always be an ever more to incarnate. This ever more is the very meaning of evolution and the misunderstood "God" we pursue in an orangutan form, a religious or a scientific form; although if we did not baptize Him, He might be the better for it, and we too. But it is one and the same Thing, there, always there – only, there are points of rupture among the species, moments of access to another state or another relation. It is quite evident that on its own a chameleon could not imagine (provided it does imagine) anything other than a superchameleon endowed with more lavish colors and more skillful predatory capabilities; similarly, a queen mole would enlarge its storehouse and tunnels – which is what we are doing in our human way. What, then, is that "vanishing point" to something else, that "moment of imagination" when we emerge into an elsewhere that was always there, another thing that was the same thing, seen and appropriated differently?

If we are to believe materialistic mechanics, nothing can come out of a system except what is already contained in it; we can only perfect what is there, in the little bubble. In a sense, they are right, but one may wonder if a perfected ass will ever yield anything other than an ass. It would seem that the closed system of the materialists is doomed to ultimate poverty, and that, by reducing everything to the degree of development of chromosomes and the perfection of gray matter, they have dedicated themselves to a supermechanization of the machine from which they started (machinery can only lead to machinery). But the ape, the mole and the chameleon do just that; they add and subtract; and our machinery is not fundamentally more advanced than theirs, even though it sends firecrackers to the moon. In short, we are some perfected protoplasm with greater swallowing capacity and smarter (?) tropisms, and soon we shall be able to calculate all that is required to produce biological Napoleons and test-tube Einsteins. All the same, our earth would hardly be a happier place with legions of blackboards and supergenerals, who would not know which way to turn – they would set out to colonize other earths . . . and fill them with blackboards. There is no way out of it, by definition, since the system is closed, closed, closed.

We suggest that there is a better materialism, less impoverishing, and that matter is less stupid than is usually said. Our materialism is a relic of the age of religions, one could almost say its inevitable companion, like good and evil, black and white, and all the dualities stemming from a linear vision of the world which sees one tuft of grass after another, a bump after a hole, and sets the mountains against the plains, without realizing that everything together is equally and totally true and makes a perfect geography in which there is not a single hole to fill, a single bump to take away, without impoverishing all the rest. There is nothing to suppress; there is everything to view in the global truth. There are no contradictions; there are only limited visions. We thus claim that matter – our matter – is capable of greater wonders than all the mechanical miracles we try to wrest from it. Matter is not coerced with impunity. It is more conscious than we believe, less closed than our mental fortress – it goes along for a while, because it is slow, then takes its revenge, mercilessly. But one has to know the right lever. We have tried to find that lever by dissecting it scientifically or religiously; we have invented microscopes and scalpels, and still more microscopes that probed deeper, saw bigger, and discovered a smaller and smaller and still smaller reality, which always seemed to be the coveted key but merely opened the door onto another, smaller existence, endlessly pushing back the limits enclosed in other limits that enclosed other limits – and the key kept escaping us, even as it let loose a few monsters on us in the process. We peered at an ant that was growing bigger and bigger but kept perpetually having six legs despite the superacids and superparticles we discovered in its ant belly. Perhaps we will be able to manufacture another one, even a three-legged ant. Some break-through! We do not need another ant, even an improved one. We need something else. Religiously, too, we have tried to dissect matter, to reduce it to a fiction of God, a vale of transit, a kingdom of the devil and the flesh, the thousand and one particles of our theological telescopes. We peered higher and higher into heaven, more and more divinely, but the ant kept painfully having six legs—or three—between one birth and another, eternally the same. We do not need an ant's salvation; we need something other than an ant. Ultimately, we may not need to see bigger or higher or farther, but simply here, under our nose, in this small living aggregate which contains its own key, like the lotus seed in the mud, and to pursue a third path, which is neither that of science nor that of religion—although it may one day combine both within its rounded truth, with all our whites and blacks, goods and evils, heavens and hells, bumps and holes, in a new human or superhuman geography that all these goods and evils, holes and bumps were meticulously and accurately preparing.

This new materialism has a most powerful microscope: a ray of truth that does not stop at any appearance but travels far, far, everywhere, capturing the same "frequency" of truth in all things, all beings, under all the masks or scrambling interferences. It has an infallible telescope: a look of truth that meets itself everywhere and knows, because it *is* what it touches. But that truth has first to be unscrambled in ourselves before it can be unscrambled everywhere; if the medium is clear, everything is clear. As we have said, man has a self of fire in the center of his being, a little flame, a pure cry of being under the ruins of the machine. This fire is the one that clarifies. This fire is the one that sees. For it is a fire of truth in the center of the being, and there is one and the same Fire everywhere, in all beings and all things and all movements of the world and the stars, in this pebble beside the path and that winged seed wafted by the wind. Five thousand years ago the Vedic Rishis were already singing its praises: "O Fire, that splendour of thine, which is in heaven and which is in the earth and in growths and its waters . . . is a brilliant ocean of light in which is divine vision . . .[9] He is the child of the waters, the child of the forests, the child of things stable and the child of things that move. Even in the stone he is there for man, he is there in the middle of his house . . .[10] O Fire . . . thou art the navel-knot of the earths and their inhabitants."[11] That fire the Rishis had discovered five thousand years before the scientists – they had found it even in water. They called it "the third fire," the one that is neither in the flame nor in lightning: *saura agni*, the solar fire,* the "sun in darkness."[12] And they found it solely by the power of direct vision of Truth, without instruments, solely by the knowledge of their own inner Fire – from the like to the like. While through their microscopes the scientists have only discovered the material support – the atom – of that fundamental Fire which is at the heart of

---

* It was not until 1938 and the cycle of Bethe that this "third fire" – the one triggered in nuclear reactions – was discovered; and it is indeed the fire of the sun, whose enormous radiant energy results from the fusion of hydrogen nuclei into helium. Before then, science knew only of the first two kinds of fire: the fire in chemical reactions, when molecules are destroyed and recombined without any change in the structure of the constituent atoms, and the fire resulting from modifications in the atom's outer layers (the electrons), which are the source of all the electromagnetic phenomena. (Note compiled by P.B. Saint-Hilaire)

things and the beginning of the worlds. They have found the effect, not the cause. And because they have found only the effect, the scientists do not have the true mastery, or the key to transforming matter—our matter—and making it yield the real miracle that is the goal of all evolution, the "point of otherness" that will open the door to a new world.

It is this Fire that is the power of the worlds, the original igniter of evolution, the force in the rock, the force in the seed, the force "in the middle of the house." This is the lever, the seer, the one that can break the circle and all the circles of our successive thralldoms—material, animal, vital and mental. No species, even pushed to its extreme of efficiency and intelligence and light, has the power to transcend its own limits—not the chameleon, not the ape, not man—by the fiat of its improved chromosomes alone. It is only this Fire that can. This is the point of otherness, the supreme moment of imagination that sets fire to the old limits, as one day a similar supreme moment of imagination lit one and the same fire in the heart of the worlds and cast that solar seed upon the waters of time, and all those waves, those circles around it, to help it grow better, until each rootlet, each branch and twig of the great efflorescence is able to attain its own infinite, delivered by its very greatness.

And we return again to our question: What is this new consciousness? Where did it come from if it is not the fruit of our precious brain? . . . At bottom, the dread of the materialist is to find himself suddenly face to face, without warning, with a God to adore, and we certainly sympathize with him when we see the puerile pictures the religions have painted of Him. The apes, too, if they had such an idea, would have painted as childish a picture of the supernatural and divine powers of man. Is to be worshipped what makes us wider, more beautiful, more sunlit; and ultimately, that wideness, beauty and sunlight are accessible to us only because they are already there in us, otherwise we would not recognize them. Only the like recognizes the like. This growing likeness is the only godhead worthy of worship. But we want to believe that it does not stop with the gilded mediocrity of our scientific feats, any more than it stopped with the prowess of the Pithecanthropus. This "new" consciousness is therefore not so new; it is our look which is new, the likeness which is growing more perfect (we should perhaps say the world's exactitude which is drawing closer). This world, as we now all know, is not as it appears; this matter, so solid to our eyes, this water so crystalline, this exquisite rose vanish into something else, and the rose never was rose, nor the water crystalline; this water flows and bubbles as much as this table and this rock, and nothing is immobile. We have widened our field of vision. But what destroyed the rose? Which is right, the microscope or our eyes? Probably both, and neither completely. The microscope neither cancels nor negates our superficial vision; it only touches another degree of reality, a second level of the same thing. And because the microscope sees differently, it can act differently and open up to us a whole spectrum of rays that are going to change our surface. But there may be a third, unexplored level of the same eternal Thing—yet another look, for what is new under the stars except our look at the stars? And most likely there are still more levels, infinitely more levels awaiting our discovery, for what could possibly put a final stop to the great efflorescence? There is no stop, no distant Goal; there is our growing look and a Goal which is here at each instant. There is a great blossoming gradually stripping its marvel, petal by petal. And each new look changes our world and all the surface laws as drastically as the laws of Einstein have changed Newton's world. To see differently is to be able to do differently. That third level is the new consciousness. And it cancels neither the rose nor the microscope—nothing is canceled in the end, except, gradually, our folly. It only links that rose to the great total blossoming, and that bubbling water, that chance pebble, that little being alone in his corner, to the great flow of the one and only Power which gradually molds us into the golden likeness of a great inner Look. And perhaps it will open for us the door to less monstrous miracles: tiny natural miracles that bring the great Goal alive at each instant and reveal the totality of the marvel in one point.

But where is the mysterious key to that third level? In reality, it is not mysterious at all, although it is full of mysteries. It does not depend on complicated instruments, does not hide under a secret knowledge, does not fall from the sky for the elect—it is there, almost visible to the naked eye, utterly simple and natural. It has been there since the beginning of time, in that seed harboring a smoldering fire: a need to reach out and take; in that great nebula gathering its grains of atoms: a need to grow and be; under those sleeping waters already simmering with an impatient fire of life: a need for air and open space. And everything began to move, impelled by the same fire: the heliotrope toward the sun, the dove toward its companion and man toward we know not what. An immense Need in the heart of the worlds, all the way to the galaxies out there, to the limits of Andromeda, which drew each other into a mortal gravitational embrace. That need we see at our own level; it is small or less small, it asks for air or sunlight, a companion and children, books, art and music, objects by the millions— but it has really only one object, it asks for only one music, a single sun and a single air. It is a need for infi-

nity. For it was born out of infinity. And so long as it does
not meet its one object, it will not stop, nor will the galaxies stop devouring each other, nor men struggling and
toiling to seize the one thing they think they do not have,
but which pushes and prods inside, poking its unsatisfied
fire until we attain the ultimate satisfaction – and at once
the plenitude of millions of vain objects, of an ephemeral
rose and a trivial little gesture. It is this Fire that is the
key, because it is born out of the supreme Power that set
the world on fire; it is this Fire that sees, because it is
born out of the supreme Vision that conceived this seed;
it is this Fire that knows, because it recognizes itself
everywhere, in things and beings, in the pebble and the
stars. This is the Fire of the new world which burns in
the heart of man, "This that wakes in the sleepers," says
the Upanishad.[13] And it will not rest until everything is
restored to its full truth, and the world to its joy, for it is
born of Joy and for Joy.

But, at first, this self of fire is mixed with its obscure
undertakings; it toils and desires, struggles and strains; it
crawls with the worm, sniffs the wind for the scent of its
prey. It has to keep alive, to survive. It feels the world
with its small antennae; it sees in fragments, according to
its needs. In man, the conscious animal, it widens its
scope; it still feels, adds up its pieces, systematizes its
data: it makes laws, scholarly treatises, gospels. Yet,
behind, there is that self of fire pushing, the something
that will not quit, that grows impatient with laws and
systems and gospels, that senses a wall behind each captured truth, each framed law, that senses a trap closing
on each discovery, as if capturing were to be captured,
trapped; there is the something that directs the antenna,
which grows impatient even with the antenna, impatient
with levers and all the machinery for apprehending the
world, as if that machinery and that antenna and that

look draped one last veil over the world and prevented it from attaining its naked reality. There is that cry of being in the depths which yearns to see, which really so much needs to see and come out in the open at last: the master of the antenna and not its slave. As if, really, a master had been confined there forever, arduously casting out its pseudopods, its tentacles and all its multicolored nets to try to join with the outside. Then, one day, under the pressure of that fire of need, the machinery begins to crack. Everything cracks: laws, gospels, knowledge and all the jurisprudence of the world. We've had enough! Even of the best we've had enough. It is still a prison, a trap—thoughts, books, art and our-Father-which-art-in-heaven. Something else, something else! Oh, something we so much need, which is without a name, except for its blind need! . . . So we demechanize with the same fury with which we had mechanized. Everything is burned, nothing is left, save that pure fire. That fire which does not know, does not see anything, nothing at all anymore, not even the little fragments it had so conscientiously gathered together. It is an almost painful fire. It struggles and toils and searches and bumps into things; it wants truth, it wants the other thing, as once it wanted objects, the millions of objects of this world, and strained to get. And little by little, everything is consumed. Even the desire for the other thing, even the hope of ever clasping that impossible pure truth, even personal effort melts away; everything slips between our fingers.

A pure little flame is left.

A flame that does not know, does not see, but is. And there is a sort of softness in simply being that flame, that tiny little flame without object—it is, it simply is, purely. It even looks as if it did not need anything else. We sink into it, live in it; it is like a love for nothing, for everything. And sometimes we plunge very deeply into it;

then, all the way at the end of this tranquil fire—so tranquil—we seem to glimpse a childlike smile, something that looks transparently at the world; and, if we do not pay attention, that look is suddenly dispersed, flows with things, breathes with the plant, goes off into infinity everywhere, smiles in this one, smiles in that one, and everything becomes immediate. There is nothing to take anymore, nothing to seize, nothing to want. It is there; everything is there! It is there everywhere. A look without walls, a vision that does not bind, a knowledge that takes nothing—everything is known, instantly known. And it goes through things effortlessly, like quicksilver, light as pollen, free as the wind, smiling at everything as if we were smiling at ourselves behind everything. Where is "the other," the not-me, the outside, the inside, the near, the far? It merges with everything, communicates instantly, as if it were the same thing everywhere. And soon this little flame begins to recognize its own world; the new geography begins to take on relief, hues, variations. It is one and the same thing, and yet each thing looks unique; there is one and the same fire, but each fire has a particular intensity, a special frequency, a dominant vibration and a seemingly totally different music. Each being has its music, each thing its rhythm, each moment its color, each event its cadence, and everything begins to be tied together. Everything takes on another meaning, a kind of total meaning in which each minute performer has its irreplaceable role, its unique presence, its unique note, its indispensable gesture. Then a vast, miraculous unfolding begins to take place before our eyes. The world is a miracle—a discovery at every step, a revelation of a microscopic order, an infinite journey into the finite. We are in the new consciousness; we have seized the fire of the new world: "O Fire . . . thou art the supreme growth and expansion of our being, all glory and beauty are in thy desirable hue and thy perfect vision. O Vastness, thou are the plenitude that carries us to the end of our way; thou art a multitude of riches spread out on every side."[14]

8

The Change of Vision

THIS CHANGE of vision is not spectacular or immediate; it is produced by small drops of a new outlook one hardly knows is a new outlook. One walks right past it, perhaps not unlike the caveman who walks past a gold nugget, glances at it because it glitters, and throws it away. Gold? What use is gold? We have to walk by the same futile point again and again, which does glitter a little and has a special something about it, before we understand that gold is gold – we have to invent gold; we have to invent the whole world and find what is already there. The difficulty is not in discovering hidden secrets but in discovering the visible, and that unsuspected gold in the midst of banality – actually, there is no banality; there is only unconsciousness. There is an age-old habit of looking at the world in relation to our needs and with respect to ourselves, like the logger in the forest who sees rosewood and only rosewood. Some measure of "eccentricity" is necessary to make the discovery. And in the end we realize that that eccentricity is the first step to a truer centricity and the key to a whole new set of relations. Our forest becomes stocked with a variety of unknown trees, and everything is a discovery.

We have also been biased by what we could call the "visionary's tradition." It has always seemed that the privileged among men were the ones who had "visions," who could see our everyday grayness in pink and green and blue, see apparitions and supernatural phenomena — a sort of supercinema one enjoys free of charge in the privacy of one's own room by pressing the psychic button. And that is all very well, there's nothing to say, but experience shows that this sort of vision changes absolutely nothing. Tomorrow millions of men could be given the power of vision by a stroke of grace, and they would turn on their little psychic television again and again; they would see gods laden with gold (and perhaps a few hells more in accord with their natural affinities), flowers more magnificent than any rose (and a scattering of awesome serpents), flying or haloed beings (but devils imitate halos very well, they are more showy than the gods, they like tinsel), landscapes of "dream," sumptuous fruits, crystal dwellings — but in the end, after the hundredth time, they would be as bored as before and leap avidly at the six-o'clock news. Something is sorely wanting in all that supernatural fireworks. And, to tell the truth, that something is everything. If our natural does not become truer, no amount of supernatural will remedy it; if our inner dwelling is ugly, no miraculous crystal will ever brighten our day, no fruit will ever quench our thirst. Unless Paradise is established on earth, it will never be anywhere. For we take ourselves everywhere we go, even into death, and so long as this "stupid" second is not filled with heaven, no eternity will ever be lit with any star. The transmutation must take place in the body and in everyday life; otherwise no gold will ever glitter, here or anywhere else, for ages of ages. What matters is not to see in pink or green or gold, but to see the truth of the world, which is so much more marvelous than any paradise, artificial or not, because the earth, this very small earth among millions of planets, is the experimental site where the supreme Truth of all the worlds has chosen to incarnate in what seems to be its very contradiction, and, by virtue of this very contradiction, to become all-light in darkness, all-breadth in narrowness, immortality in death, and living plenitude in each atom at each instant.

But we have to collaborate.

The seeker of the truth of the earth constantly encounters this "contradiction." And that is the key to the new vision. He encounters it in himself, in others, in circumstances: nothing "works" as it should. Where is the truth in this chaos, confusion, falsehood? Not here, to be sure; we must struggle, reject, correct circumstances, strive towards a something that is out there, in the distance, tomorrow or the day after. And truth keeps eluding us completely. Others before us have "corrected circumstances"—in Babylon, in Thebes, in Kapilavastu. For the past ten thousand years we have gone through one civilization after another, and it is certainly an illusion to believe that ours will not go, and that the Western world, with all its scientific and cultural truths, will forever remain the center of the world. For, actually, tomorrow or the day after *never* comes. If truth is not right here now, it will never be. That is the simple mathematics of the world.

Truth is totally natural, which is why we do not see it. It is even the most natural thing in the world. It was there from the very first blast of atoms, otherwise when would it have ever appeared, at what period of Andromeda, the Crab or the local galaxy we live in, brought by what prophet, what discovery, what miracle? Prophets have come and gone; discovery is added to discovery and today's miracles will form archeological strata for the citizens of another era. We aren't there yet, and yet we have always been there, in the midst of the miracle. Only, there is a moment when one opens one's eyes to the miracle. And that is the only moment in the world, the Great Moment of all ages and all earths – for everything is tied together, there is but one body in the world and but one look for all the universes. We cannot change one point of the world without changing everything, open our eyes here without opening them there, touch one center of truth without touching them all, instantly, regardless of distance, because there is but one Truth and one center.

Is this to say that nobody has ever touched this Truth? Of course it has been touched, but on the mental heights, in rare illuminations that left a trace here or there, on a Buddha's face in Indonesia, an Athena in the Parthenon, a smile in Rheims, in some marvelous Upanishads, a few words of grace that have survived as a golden and adorable anachronism, hardly real amidst our concrete structures and civilized savagery; it has been touched in the depths of the heart, stammered out by Saint Francis of Assisi or Sri Ramakrishna. But then the world goes on, and we all know that the last word belongs to the bomb and to the triumph of the latest democratic hero, who will soon join another one under the same layer of inanity. But it has never been touched in matter; it has never been touched there. And so long as it is not touched there, it will remain what it has always been, a brilliant dream over the chaos of the ages, and the world will go on whirling vainly, adding its discoveries that discover nothing and its pseudo-knowledge that always ends up stifling us. Indeed, we labor under a bizarre delusion: we right a wrong here only to cause another one to sprout there; we seal a crack here only to see the wound open wider somewhere else. And it is always the same wound; there is only one wound in the world, and so long as we do not want to be cured of that ill, our millions of drugs and parliaments and systems and laws – millions of laws, on every street corner and right in our mailbox – will never cure us or the world's illness. We philanthropize and altruize, we distribute and share and equalize; but our good deeds seem to go hand in hand with our misdeeds, and the misery, the great misery of the world, infiltrates everything and gnaws surreptitiously at our functional homes and empty hearts; our equalizations are the huge, gray uniformity that descends upon the earth, smothering equally the good and the less good, the rich and the poor, the crowds from here or there – the great mechanized human crowd, disincarnate, manipulated by a thousand radios and newspapers that scream and rumble all the way up to Himalayan villages. And no news at all. Not a single bit of news in those billions of novelties! Not an iota of novelty under the stars: men suffer and die in their superhospitals that cure nothing and in their supercities teeming with mental disorders. But tomorrow will be better, we think, with more machines, more drugs, more red or blue or green crosses, more laws and still more laws to remedy the world's cancer. And we seem to hear, from far, far away in the past, six thousand years in the past, the moving little voice of Lopamudra, the wife of Rishi Agastya: "Many autumns have I toiled night and day; the dawns age me, age dims the glory of our bodies . . .,"[15] and that of Maitreya echoing her: "What shall I do with that by which the nectar of Immortality is not attained?"[16]

Does this mean that we have not progressed? We certainly have not progressed as we imagine. We are not any more human than the Theban or the Athenian, no more "advanced" than they despite all our machines. As Sri Aurobindo put it, "Machinery is necessary to modern

humanity because of our incurable barbarism."[17] We
think we have mastered, but we have mastered nothing
at all! Our machines are a testimony to our impotence, a
huge prosthesis to correct our incapacity to see far, hear
far, penetrate the heart of things and understand instantly
and directly. We do not know any better now than ten
thousand years ago how to modify matter through will-
power (perhaps we even knew it better then), how to
illuminate with consciousness and understand through
vision. Under all our apparatus, we are less advanced
than the animal with its sixth sense and the pygmy of
Central Africa. Our machines see better than we, feel
better than we, count better than we, and perhaps they
will end up living better than we. Matter escapes us completely. It takes a simple power failure for us to revert to
the caveman. For progress is not improving the existing
world or discovering new procedures: it is a change of
consciousness and vision.

But at least we have progressed in one direction, which
is not the one we think. We have completed the cycle of
the ape; we have pushed to its ultimate consequence the
simple little gesture that tied a vine to a branch to make a
bow; we have inflated and overinflated the mental
balloon to its breaking point. And Nature's design is accomplished, which was not just to take stock of the
world, but to lead the whole species to the zero point, to
that supreme juncture where there is not a single jungle
left to explore, not one sea to plumb, not one Himalaya,
when soon not even an acre of ground will be left for our
concrete and steel structures, when even the gods have
been squeezed dry of all their juices and collect dust on
the shelves of our libraries, when life collapses under its
own weight and leaves us again, like ancient man under
the stars, alone, face to face with the mystery of the
earth, to find the name of things, their power of being,

the true vibration that dwells in us and links us to the world: the naked mystery of this unsullied moment, the original music of things, which is perhaps their ultimate truth and ultimate power, an original vision that is a new birth of the world, and perhaps the promise of its transformation. This is the end of the mental world. We are before naked matter. We are at the time of the great Invention. And we are almost ridiculously inadequate for such a fabulous adventure. What do we have? A little fire inside, whose goal we do not even know, but which burns with us, accompanies our steps, our thousands of steps in the great vain machine; a little clearing that sometimes seems so lovely and light, and so fragile in the midst of the huge empty chaos – that's all we have. It is childlike and transparent and almost ridiculous amid the strides of the caparisoned colossi of the mind. And what do we discover? A breath, a nothing, a speck of gold glittering for a moment and then vanishing. There is nothing sensational. It is the opposite of sensational; it is unassuming minuteness; it is perhaps nothing, and it is everything. It is as fluid as the man bending for the first time over the first river in the world and looking at a blade of grass pass by, and then another (come from where, carried away where?), a fugitive reflection of the sky, and that other little cascade in his heart. But it all makes a single whole, and for a fraction of a second, a sort of look opens up and pervades that drop of water and the blade of grass with infinity, and the over there it comes from and the other there it goes to, as if everything had already happened, as if nothing ever happened, nothing ever passed: an eternal meeting between that pink in the sky, this heartbeat and this frail blade of grass. And other blades of grass may come, other pinks or blues or blacks go by, but it is always the same thing meeting itself, at the same point, with other faces and other names. So, something begins to take root in this meeting point of the worlds, as if one and the same look were looking at one and the same story. And everything is tranquil, identical and clear; there is no need to strain toward tomorrow, to grasp at that pink or blue, this blade of grass or that one; there are no other points out there, or else it is the same one and the same things meeting each other; there is only one point at each instant, and the whole world passes through it, along with Sagittarius and Betelgeuse and that twig. All is contained there, for ages upon ages. We just have to listen to the music of that point to hear all other music, we just have to be there to be with all other beings, past, present and future – there is but one story in the world and one moment and one being. It is right there; we are in it. There will be nothing more, nothing else, in three thousand years or a hundred thousand.

From then on, each thing is, simply and absolutely. We are at that meeting point of being, and we look at the great world, brand new. There is no hope for anything else, no expectation, no regret or desire – if it is not there at that moment, it will never be there! Everything is there, the total totality of all possible futures. Water may flow, and the faces and thunder of the world, the costume of the moment, the cry of the passerby, the flying seed. The great kaleidoscope turns and strews beings, events, countries and their kings, and this fleeting second, colors them blue, red or gold, but there is still the same look at the meeting point, the same second and the same thing in different colors, the same beings with their sorrows, with white skin or dark, in this century or another. There is nothing new under the sun, nothing to expect! There is that one little second to delve into, delve into and deepen, to live totally, as if forever and ever; there is that unique thing that passes, that unique being, that speck of pollen

or dust, that unique happening in the world. Then everything begins to be filled with such total meaning, to extend and branch out to the four corners of the world, to
vibrate with total significance, as if this face, that chance
encounter, that passing blue or black hue, this unexpected stumbling or bird feather floating in the wind
brought us a message—each thing is a message, a sign of
our position and the position of the whole. Nothing exists
in relation to this little shadow anymore, to its needs, its
desires, its expectation of things or people—everything is
clear, everything passes through our clearing as it is,
without plus or minus, good or evil, rejection or choice or
preference or will of any kind. What could we possibly
want? We already have everything, forever. What else is
there! Each passing circumstance divulges its keynote,
its pure music, its innermost meaning, without addition
or subtraction, without false visual color—through things
and beings we watch one and the same tranquil eternity
unfolding. We are in our point of eternity, in a look of
truth. We are at that crossroads of being, which, for a
moment, seems to open innumerably upon everything.
One full little second. Where is the lack, the vain, the
missing? Where is the big, the infinite, the useful or
useless? We have arrived; we are right in *the* Thing.
There is no more "quest for rosewood" in the forest of the
great world; everything is rosewood and each thing is the
one essence. A kind of warm gold begins to glow everywhere.

And the seeker has put his finger on the fourth golden
rule of the passage: Each second totally and clearly.

*
* *

But how do those clear little seconds help change the
world? Perhaps exactly the way the brief distracted

second of the ape—distracted from its immediate interests—helped give birth to the first thought. For a whole world starts pouring into that transparency, but in imperceptible little breaths, in little drops of nothing—to be sure, the "uselessness" of things is a terrible snare, an ever-present trap, the old mistake that engulfs the world in its dark false vision. At every moment the seeker must struggle against the old way of looking, correct himself, catch himself in the act. The new vision demands a long apprenticeship. One knows neither where it leads nor its use. What was the use of the ape's reflection, except to disturb its immediate acrobatics? And yet, the seeker comes back to it, as if drawn in spite of himself; he receives little signs, demonstrations in the flesh. It is as if somebody or something were there, watching over everything and taking advantage of the least crack in the old machinery to slip in a drop of light—a hole is needed, a crack in the shell, a lapse in the old habit of being, for the new world to get in! Little by little the seeker yields. He lets himself go, he turns his look on the thousands of everyday useless things, the meaningless incidents, the senseless encounters, the multitude of microscopic "unconnected" events. He is in his fire of being and he looks; he looks at each thing as a would-be revelation, a truth concealed; and if nothing is revealed, he still persists, he observes everything, records everything: the futile steps, the useless detours, the closed faces, the accidents without reason. Instead of jumping at the desirable, he watches its movement, how it follows its course and attains its goal; instead of rejecting an unpleasant encounter, he watches it come, welcomes it, lets it give out its little drop of truth, its message beneath the falsehood or confusion; instead of running away from the darkness, evil or negation flung at him, he waits calmly for the darkness to disclose its lesson for him, the evil its drop of good beneath its venom, the negation, its vaster yes awaiting its hour. And finally he discovers a YES everywhere, a good everywhere, a meaning everywhere, and that everything is ascending, moving in the Great Direction, beneath the good and the evil, the black and the white, the useful and the harmful. Gradually, the world teems with a thousand little truths twinkling here and there, filling this vacuum, plugging that useless hole, connecting things to one another, dropping the missing piece of the jigsaw puzzle into place, and everything ties together as one continuous message—every moment things whisper in our ear and destiny speaks in a dove feather lifted by the wind. But once more we are struck by the same peculiarity. What we discover are not eternal and sublime truths, not triumphs of the geometrical mind that confines the world in an equation, not seeds of dogma or revelations atop the Sinais of the world, but minuscule little truths, vivid and light, smiles of truth along the path and in everyday commonplaceness—a minuscule, contagious truth which seems to spread from place to place and light up even the rocks: a truth of the earth, a truth of matter. And when we can trap a single one of these little whimsical smiles, we are richer than if the illuminations of all the sages put together were bestowed on us, because we have touched the truth with our eyes wide open and with our body—maybe because the Supreme Truth is also there, in an infinitesimal wisp of straw as much as in the totality of all the ages.

But, beyond all meanings being released from their hiding place, the seeker touches upon an even greater mystery, something so elusive and so strong, which makes his heart flutter every time he thinks he has caught a glimpse of it—oh, something that is well hidden, that will not let itself be caught and put into thoughts or mental ciphers: a supreme Cipher that deciphers all and is like the true key to the new world. Behind all his gropings and stumblings and dozens of wrong turns every day, his cries in the dark, he senses a sort of Help — something is *answering*. . . . One must have walked long in the dark to appreciate the marvel of that particular answer. Something answers, moves, hears, knows where we are going! As if the new world were all here, already done, innumerably mapped under our steps and under each step of each being at each instant — and we gradually enter its geography. This is really the sign of the new world: it is here; there is no distance to travel, no waiting in prayer, no cry to echo across empty spaces in order to seduce the godhead veiled in the clouds, no intensity of concentration, no long-drawn-out years or protracted efforts or arduous repetitions to try to move a deaf Force — it is here, the instantaneous answer, the boon in the flesh, the vital sign, the living demonstration. It takes but a simple call. It takes but a little cry of pure truth. Actually, we do not seek; we are sought. We do not call; we are called. We grope about only as long as we want to do everything by ourselves. There is nothing to do! There is everything to undo, and let the new world flow freely, let its unexpected rivers and paths run under our steps. One brief second of abandon, and it comes in; it is there, smiling. Everything is already there! When the ape felt he was exerting himself so much to capture a subtle little vibration, when he caught hold of a thought by chance, without knowing how or why, at the moment when his simian machinery was not working as usual, he, too, perhaps was walking in a new mental geography that was waiting for his lapses of apehood and a brief second of abandon to the mystery of the new world. We think that everything comes out of our wonderful brains, but we are the tools of a greater self, the translators of an approaching marvel, the transmitters of a growing music. But the music must be allowed to flow freely; the instrument must be clear.

And it is conceivable that if the world tuned its instrument to this other music, it would find itself radically changed.

9

The Greater Self

WHAT IS this greater self?

In fact, the self has always been great. We might as well ask, "What is this greater moon?" Because we see a first quarter and then a second, we say, with our geocentric vision, that the moon grows bigger. Our eyes see one thing after another, and for them things grow bigger or appear—unless we are still childish enough to claim they fall from the sky or are eaten by dragons. Things and beings "die," we think, carried away, like the moon, by the dragon of death, but they are still there, just hidden from our vision, and nothing ever dies or disappears, any more than anything ever gets born or appears, like the full moon and the new moon. There is merely something eclipsing our vision. And when we say that this lesser or greater self is the result of our lesser or greater capacities, we may be as vain as the savage looking through a telescope for the first time and saying that those unknown stars and lights blinking at the edge of the universe are the result of our instruments. The world does not "arrive" and nothing arrives; it is we who gradually arrive at total vision. And the fuller that vision, the more the world attains the perfection it has always been.

But what eclipses our vision? We might as well ask, "What eclipses the linear vision of the centipede?" Or what eclipses the lotus in the seed? For our eyes, the universe is gradually becoming, but our eyes are really the supreme Look hiding from itself to look through the eternity of the ages and through our millions of eyes, and with millions of colors and faces, at the one perfection it saw in an eternal white second. The world is *one*; it is a single global unity, even the scientists tell us so. And they are trying to find that equation. But to restore this oneness, they have divided and subdivided matter to infinity, or almost. They have come upon an infinitesimal existence and a smaller infinitesimal existence, a vastness and an even greater vastness. But this oneness is neither an addition nor a reduction to the microscopic level, any more than eternity is an infinite number of years or immensity so many miles plus one. This oneness is there, totally, in each point of space and at each second of time, as much as in all the infinitudes put together and all the vastness added up. Each point contains the whole; each second is eternity looking at itself. And we who stand in this point at this second are eternal and complete, and all the earths and all the galaxies meet in our essential point; an eternal lotus shines in our heart—only we do not know it. We know it little by little. And it is not enough to know it in our heads and hearts—we have to know it in our body. Then the marvel will be truly complete and the eternal lotus on the summits of the spirit will shine forever in our matter and in each second of time.

This perfection, this oneness of substance and consciousness and being, is like the world's golden memory, the blurred image that each one and each thing strives to conjure up and capture, the goad of the world's great Thirst, the driving force of its gigantic Need to be and

embrace and grow. It is like a tenacious memory thrusting things and beings and even galaxies into a mortal
embrace that would like to be an embrace of love, that
would like to understand all, hold and possess and en-
compass all within its circumference. Each thing strives
toward that gropingly: the sea anemone with its tentacles, the atom with its gravitation, and man with his intelligence and his heart. But our thirst cannot be quenched
until it seizes all, encompasses all in its being, and there
remains not one particle of the universe that has not
become our substance, for, in reality, everything was
always our substance and our being and our own face
under millions of smiles or sufferings seeking their
smile — but which cannot really smile so long as they have
not found what they always were. There is no other suffering in the world, no other gap, no other lack. But so
long as this need is not fulfilled, we will go on and on;
atoms will go on whirling to make increasingly purer and
lighter kinds of matter, sea anemones ceaselessly seizing
and men adding up their treasures, plundering or loving —
but only one thing is lovable, and until they love everything, they will love nothing really and will possess only
their shadow.

But how is it that this self, this great self that we are,
divided itself, multiplied, atomized into a million things
and beings? Why the long journey of repossession?
Actually, it did not really divide; it was never pulverized
into stars separated by light-years, into amoebas of consciousness separated by teguments, rinds or armor of being, into little men separated from each other by a white
skin or black and a few vague thoughts. Nothing was
ever separated and our stars meet in one single little star
that shines in the heart of man and in each thing and each
pebble of the universe. How could we ever recognize the
world if we were not already it? We can only know what

we are, and anything that is not us is simply nonexistent or invisible to our eyes. We can foresee tomorrow, sense an accident coming, a pain or a thought ten thousand miles away, a treasure buried in a field, the tiny life quivering in a leaf in front of us only because we are connected; we are one, and everything is already there, immediately and without separation – tomorrow and the day after, the here and there, in sight and out of sight. There is no separation; there are only eyes that do not see well. There is a sum of invisible things that gradually become visible, from the protoplasm to the caterpillar to man, and we have not exhausted the whole spectrum. Tomorrow, perhaps, we shall see that the distance between one country and another, one being and another, between today and tomorrow is as fragile and illusory as the tuft of grass separating one caterpillar from another in the same field. And we shall step over the wall of time and space as today we step over the caterpillar's tuft of grass.

We have cut little pieces out of that great indivisible oneness, that fullness of the world, that global self. We have sliced little pieces out of space and time, particles of self and not-self, protons and electrons, pluses and minuses tightly wedded to one another, good and evil, night and day inextricably bound to one another, incomplete without one another, never complete with each other; for all the nights and days together will never make a complete day; all the pluses and minuses, goods and evils, selves and not-selves added up will never make a full beauty, a single being. And we have replaced oneness by multiplicity, love by loves, rhythm by harmonies that are broken and restored. But our fusion is nothing but an addition, and life is born out of death as if we constantly had to destroy in order to be, split in order to join in a new appearance of unity – which is only the sum of the same separations, of the same good and evil, of plus and minus, of a self that is a million past selves but not a single little full drop. We have drawn a little circle in the great indivisible Life, enclosed a fragment of being in a gelatine capsule, set apart one note of the great rhythm beneath a shell of beast or man, and seized a few hard and trenchant thoughts from the great rainbow current whose strands dangled over the bushes of the world. We have cut up the great Look in the heart of things and produced a thousand irreducible facets. And since we could no longer see anything of the great world, shielded, fragmented and syncopated as it was, we have invented eyes to see what we had driven away, ears to hear what whispered everywhere, fingers to grasp a few fragments of a full beauty we had truncated, and thirst, desire, hunger for everything that was no longer us—antennas, thousands of antennas to capture the one note that would fill our hearts. And since we could no longer grasp anything without these inventions, these eyes, senses and gray cells—oh, so gray!—we came to believe that the world was inaccessible without them, that it resembled the reading on our little dials, and that perhaps we were even the creators of the broken waves going through our antennas. We have said I, others, and I again and I forever and ever, in a black or a yellow skin, under an Athenian shell or a Theban one, under these ruins or those, under the same old ruins of little I's who die without knowing why, who live by fragments, enjoy themselves without ever really enjoying themselves, and come back again and again to understand what they had not understood and, perhaps, to build the full City of the great self at last. When we touch that fullness, our good will no longer clash with our evil, our pluses with our minuses, because everything will be our good and flow in the same direction; our nights will no longer be the opposite of our days, our loves a fraction of all loves, our little notes a cry torn from the great Note, because there will be only one music playing through our millions of instruments, only one love with a million faces and only one great day with its cool shades and rainbow cascades beneath the great tree of the world. Then it may become unnecessary to die, because we will have found the secret of the life that is reborn from its own joy – one dies only from lack of joy and in order to find an ever greater joy.

*
* *

This all, this great all has been seen by sages in their visions and by a few rare poets and thinkers: "All this is Brahman immortal, naught else; Brahman is in front of us, Brahman behind us, to the south of us and to the north of us and below us and above us; it stretches everywhere. All this is Brahman alone, all this magnificent universe."[18] "Thou art woman and thou art man also; Thou art the boy and girl, and Thou art yonder worn and aged man that walkest bending upon a staff. . . . Thou art the blue bird and the green and the scarlet- eyed."[19] "Thou art That, O Swetaketu."[20] This great all that is us has shined at the summit of human accomplishment, left a few hieroglyphic traces on the walls of Thebes, and nourished initiates here and there – at times we have entered a white radiance above the worlds where, in a flash, we have dissolved the little self and emerged into a cosmic consciousness. . . . But none of that has changed the world. We still did not have the clue that would connect that vision to this earth and make a new world with a new look. Our truths remained fragile; the earth remained refractory – and rightly so. Why should it obey the illuminations from above if that light does not affect its matter, if it itself does not see and it itself is not illuminated? In truth, wisdom is very wise and the earth's darkness is not a negation of the Spirit, any more than night is a negation of day; it is an expectation and a calling for light, and so long as we do not call the light *here*, why should it trouble itself to move from its summits? So long as we do not turn our nocturnal half toward its sun, why should it be filled with light? If we seek solar wholeness on the summits of the mind, we shall have wholeness there, in a lovely thought; if we seek it in the heart, we shall have it there, in a tender emotion—if we seek it in matter at every instant, we shall have that same wholeness in matter and at every instant of matter. We have to know where we are looking. We cannot reasonably find the light where we are not looking. Then, perhaps, we shall realize that this earth was not so dark after all. It was our look that was dark, our want of being that brought about the want of things. The earth's resistance is our own resistance—and the promise of a solid truth: an innumerable bursting of rainbows into incarnate myriads instead of an empty radiance on the heights of the Spirit.

But the seeker of the new world has not pursued his quest in a straight line; he has not closed his doors, rejected matter, muffled his soul. He has taken his quest along wherever he went, on the boulevards and on the stairways, in the crowd and in the empty obscurity of millions of senseless gestures. He has pervaded all the wastelands with being, kindled his fire in all the vanities, and fed his need on the very inanity that stifled him. He was not a little one-pointed concentration that rose straight up to the heights and then fell asleep in the white peace of the spirit; he was this chaos and turmoil, this wandering back and forth, in nothing. He pulled all into his net—the ups and downs, the blacks and less blacks and so-called whites, the falls and setbacks—he held everything within his little circumference, with a fire at the center, a need for truth amid this chaos, a cry for help in this nothingness. He was a tangled course, an endless meandering of which he knew nothing, except that he carried his fire there – his fire for nothing, for everything. He no longer even expected anything from anything; he was only like a mellowness of burning, as if that fire were the goal in itself, the being amid all this emptiness, the only presence in this enormous absence. It even ended up becoming a sort of quiet love, for nothing, for everything, here and there. And little by little, this nothingness was lit up; this emptiness was set afire by his look; this futility stirred with the same little warmth. And everything began to answer. The world came to life everywhere, shining everywhere, in the black and the white, the high and the low. It was like a birth everywhere, but infinitesimal, microscopic: a powdering of little truths dancing here and there, in facts and gestures, in things and meetings – it even seems as if they came to meet him. It was a strange multiplication, a kind of golden contagion.

Gradually, he entered an all, but, oh, quite an odd "all," which had nothing to do with a cosmic or transcendent or dazzling consciousness – yet which was like a million little bursts of gold, fleeting, elusive, almost mocking. Perhaps we should say "a microscopic consciousness"? – and warm: a sudden sweetness of recognition, an eruption of gratefulness, an incomprehensible flush of tenderness, as if it were living, vibrating, responding in every corner and every direction. Strangely, when a question arose, or a doubt, or an uncertainty about something or someone, a problem about a course of action, an anxiety about what to do or not to do, it seemed as if the answer came to him *as living facts* – not as an illumination or inspiration, a revelation or thought, nothing of that sort: a material answer in external circumstances, as though the earth itself, life itself, supplied the answer. As if the very circumstances came and took his hand and said, "Here, you see?" And not great circumstances, not sensational flashes: very little facts, while going from one end of the street to the other. All of a sudden the thing came to him, the person or the encounter, the money, the book, or the unexpected development – the living answer. Or, on the contrary, when he was so much hoping for certain news (if he had not yet been cured of the disease of hope), when he was looking forward to some arrangement, a peaceful retreat, a clear-cut solution, he was suddenly engulfed in a still greater chaos, as if everything turned against him – people, things, circumstances – or he fell ill, met with an "accident," opened the door to an old weakness and seemed to be treading the old road of suffering again. Then, two hours or two days or two months later, he realized that that adversity was exactly what was needed, which led, by a circuitous route, to a goal larger than he had foreseen; that that illness had purified his substance, cut him off from a wrong course, and brought him back, lighter, onto the sunlit path; that that fall had exposed old hiding places in himself and clarified his heart; that that unfortunate encounter was a perfection of exactness to bring forth a whole new network of possibilities or impossibilities to overcome; and that everything concurred meticulously to prepare his strength, his breadth, his extreme swiftness, through a thousand and one detours – the all prepared him for the all. He then begins to experience a succession of unbelievable little miracles, of strange happenings, bewildering coincidences . . . as if, really, everything knew, each thing knew what it had to do and went straight to its microscopic goal amidst millions of passersby and trifling events. At first, the seeker does not believe it; he shrugs his shoulders and dismisses it, then he opens one eye, then the other, and doubts his own amazement. It is of such microscopic exactness, such fabulously unbelievable precision in the midst of this gigantic crisscrossing of lives and things and circumstances, that it is simply impossible — it is like an explosion of total knowledge embracing in one fell swoop this ant walking down Main Street and the thousands of passersby and all their possible itineraries, all their particular circumstances — past, present and future — to create this unique conjunction, this incredible perfect little second in which everything accords and agrees, *is* inevitably, and provides the unique answer to a unique question.

And the same things happens again and again; the "coincidences" multiply. Chance gradually reveals an innumerable smile — or, perhaps, another self, a great self, which knows its totality, and each fragment of its totality and each second of its world, as much as our body knows the least quiver of its cells, and the passing fly, and the rhythm of its heart. With eyes wide open, the seeker begins to enter an innumerable wonder. The world is a single body, the earth, a single consciousness in motion. But not a body whose consciousness is centered in a few gray cells upstairs: an innumerable consciousness centered everywhere and as total in a little ephemeral cell as in the gesture that will alter the destiny of nations. In each point consciousness answers consciousness. The seeker has left the cutting little truths of the mind, the dogmatic and geometric lines of thought. He enters an inexpressible fullness of view, a comprehensive truth in which each fragment has its meaning and each second, its smile, each darkness, its light, each harshness, its awaiting sweetness. He gropingly discovers "the honeycombs covered by the rock."[21] Each fall is a degree of widening, each footstep, a blossoming of the inevitable efflorescence, each adversity, a lever of the future. Being wrong is a crack in our armor through which a flame of pure love shines which understands everything.

10

Harmony

WE MIGHT be tempted to say that these are fantasies, unbelievable miracles. But in fact it is all very simple. There are no miracles. There is a vast Harmony which governs the world with a precision and delicacy as faultless in the meeting of atoms and the cycle of flowering and the return of migrating birds as in the meeting of men and the unfolding of events at a particular juncture. There is a vast, unique movement we thought we were separated from because we had built our little mental turrets on the frontier of our comprehension and black dotted lines on the softness of a great earthly hill, as others had built their hunting grounds, and the sea gulls, their white archipelago on the foam-flecked waters. And because we had put on these blinders or others to protect ourselves from the formidable magnitude of our lands, erected these dwarf fences to farm our little acre, the little wave of energy trapped in our sails, the little golden (or less golden) fireflies caught in the net of our intelligence, the little note captured from too great a Harmony, we have thought that the world behaved according to our laws, or at least our laws to the factual wisdom of our instruments and calculations, and that anything that exceeded this partitioning of the world or slipped through the meshes was unthinkable or nonexistent, "miraculous"–hallucinatory. We were caught in our own trap. And by some gracious kindness – which is perhaps one of the greatest mysteries to elucidate – the world began to resemble our drawings of erudite children, our illnesses to follow the doctor's prognosis, our bodies to obey the prescribed medicine, our lives to travel in the designated groove between two walls of impossibility, and even our events to bow obligingly before our statistics and our thought of events. The world actually became mentalized from one end to the other and from top to bottom. Thought is the latest magician on the list, after the Mongolian shaman, the Theban occultist or the Bantu witchdoctor. It remains to be seen whether our magic is better than the others – but magic it is, and we are not yet aware of all its power. But, in truth, there is only one Power, which uses an amulet, a Tantric yantra [22] or an incantation, equally as well as a differential equation – or even our simple and futile little thought. What do we want? That is the question.

We manipulate thought haphazardly. Generally, we do not even manipulate it; it manipulates us. We are besieged by a thousand useless thoughts that run back and forth through our inner realm, automatically, futilely, ten, perhaps a hundred times by the time we have walked down the boulevard or climbed the stairs. It is hardly thought; it is a sort of thinking current that got into the habit of following some of our convolutions and circumvolutions and assumes a more or less neutral color, more or less brilliant, depending on our taste or inclination, our heredity, our environment, and is expressed by preferred or customary words, blue or gray philosophies in one language or another – but it is one and the same current running everywhere. It is the mental machinery clicking and rumbling and working sempiternally the same range or intensity of the general current. This activity veils everything, envelops everything, and casts a pall over everything with its thick and sticky cloud. But the seeker of the new world is one step removed from this machinery; he has discovered the quiet little clearing behind; he has lit a fire of need in the center of his being; he takes his fire everywhere he goes. And everything is different for him. Unclouded in his little clearing, he begins to see the functioning of the mind; he watches the great play, uncovers step by step the secrets of the mental magic – which ought perhaps to be called mental illusion, though if it is an illusion, it is a very effective one. And all sorts of phenomena begin to attract his notice, a little disorderly, in recurring little spurts that end up making a coherent picture. The more he sees, the stronger his control.

This clarity is progressive. But he does not seek to see more clearly, if we may say, because "seeking" is again to risk setting the old process in motion, enlisting the machine to fight the machine, his right hand to control his left. And, besides, we do not even know what is to be sought or found! If we set out with an "idea," we will only go in the direction of our idea, a little like the doctor locking himself (and his patient) into a diagnosis: we set up walls beforehand, a trap for something untrappable – "that" will give itself, or it won't, and that's all. The seeker (we should perhaps simply call him the one aspiring to be born) is not concerned with stopping the machinery; he is only concerned with his fire. He makes his fire burn. He is centered in that need in his depths, that poignant call for being amid the great drift, that almost painful thirst in the desert of things and beings passing by and days elapsing as though they did not exist. And his fire burns, grows hotter. And the hotter it grows, the more it consumes the machinery, dissipates the cloud, the vain thoughts, sweeps inside and out. It is the birth of the little clearing. It is the beginning of a clear little flowing that seems to vibrate behind his head, tightening his neck, sometimes even pressing hard – then he learns to let it flow freely through him, not to block the passage by resisting, to make himself supple and porous. He lets the flow fill him, the clear little vibration that seems to go on and on and flow without interruption, like a muted little song accompanying him, like a rhythm rising and pulsating endlessly, like two light bird wings beating within his innermost azure and supporting him everywhere, making a sort of tranquil sweetness of view, as though life receded, widened, sank into a clear infinity vibrating with that rhythm alone, that soft, light, transparent cadence alone. And everything starts to become extraordinarily simple.

From within that silence in him – a silence that is not empty, not an absence of noise, not a cold and toneless blank, but the smooth breadth of the open sea, an extreme of sweetness that fills him and needs neither words nor thought nor comprehension: it is instant comprehension, the embracing of everything, the absolute here and now. So what could be missing? – the seeker, the newborn to be, begins to see the mental play. First, he sees that those thousands of thoughts, gray or blue or paler, do not actually emanate from any brain. Rather, they float in midair, as it were. They are currents, vibrations, which are translated into thoughts in our heads when we capture them, as waves are translated into music or words or images in our television sets; and everything shifts and moves and whirls at different levels, flows universally over our motley little frontiers: captured in English, German, French; colored yellow, black, or blue depending on the height of our antenna;

rhythmic, broken, or scattered into a powdering of microscopic thoughts depending on our level of reception; musical, grating, or discordant depending on our clarity or complication. But the seeker, the listener, does not try to pick up one channel or another, to turn the dials of his machine to capture this or that – he is tuned in to the infinite, focused on a little flame in the center, so sweet and full, free from interference and preference. He needs only one thing: that that flame in him burn and burn, that that flowing pass again and again through his clearing, without words, without mental meaning, and yet full of meaning and of all meaning, as if it were the very source of meaning. And, at times, without his thinking or wanting it, something comes and strikes him: a little vibration, a little note alighting on his still waters and leaving a whole train of waves. And if he leans a little, to see, stretches toward that little eddy (or that slight note, that point calling out, that rip in the expanse of his being), a thought appears, a feeling, an image or a sensation – as though there were really no dividing line between one mode of translation and another; there is just something vibrating, a more or less clear rhythm, a more or less pure light being lit in him, a shadow, a heaviness, an uneasiness, sometimes a glittering little rocket, dancing and light as a powdering of sunshine on the sea, an outpouring of tenderness, a fleeting smile – and sometimes a great, solemn rhythm that seems to rise from the depths of time, immense, poignant, eternal, which calls up the unique sacred chant of the world. And It flows effortlessly. There is no need to think or want; the only need is to be and be again, to burn in unison with a single little flame that is like the very fire of the world. And, when necessary, just for a second, a little note comes knocking at his window, and there comes exactly the right thought, the impulse for the required action, the right or left turn that will open up an unexpected trail and a whole chain of answers and new opportunities. The seeker, the fervent one, then intimately understands the invocation of this five- or six-thousand-year-old Vedic poet: "O Fire, let there be created in us the correct thought that springs from Thee."[23]

But wrong thoughts, too, are a surprising source of discoveries. As a matter of fact, more and more, he realizes that this kind of distinction is meaningless. What, in the end, is not for our own good? What does not ultimately turn out to be our greater good? The wrong paths are part of the right one and pave a broader way, a larger view of our indivisible estate. The only wrong is not to see; it is the vast grayness of the *terra incognita* of our limited maps. And we indeed limit our maps. We have attributed those thoughts, feelings, reactions and desires to the little Mississippi flowing through our lands, to the thriving Potomac rivers lined with stone buildings and fortresses—and indeed, they have got into the habit of running through those channels, cascading here or there, boiling a little farther below, or disappearing into our marshes. It is a very old habit, going back even before us or the ape, or else a scarcely more recent one going back to our schooldays, our parents or yesterday's newspaper. We have opened paths, and the current follows them—it follows them obstinately. But for the demechanized seeker, the meanders and points of entry begin to become more visible. He begins to distinguish various levels in his being, various channeling centers, and when the current passes through the solar plexus or through the throat, the reactions or effects are different. But, mostly, he discovers with surprise that it is one and the same current everywhere, above or below, right or left, and those which we call "thought," "desire," "will" or "emotion" are various infiltrations of the same identical thing, which is neither thought nor desire nor will nor anything of the sort, but a trickle, a drop or a cataract of the same conscious Energy entering here or there, through our little Potomac or muddy Styx, and creating a disaster or a poem, a millipede's quiver, a revolution, a gospel or a vain thought on the boulevard – we could almost say "at will." It all depends on the quality of our opening and its level. But the fundamental fact is that this is an Energy, in other words, a Power. And thus, very simply, quite simply, we have the all-powerful source of all possible changes in the world. It is as we will it! We can tune in either here or there, create harmony or cacophony; not a single circumstance in the world, not one fateful event, not one so-called ineluctable law, absolutely nothing can prevent us from turning the antenna one way or the other and changing this muddy and disastrous flood into a limpid stream, instantly. We just have to know where we open ourselves. At every moment of the world and every second, in the face of every dreadful circumstance, every prison we have locked ourselves alive in, we can, in one stroke, with a single cry for help, a single burst of prayer, a single true look, a single leap of the little flame inside, topple all our walls and be born again from top to bottom. Everything is possible. Because that Power is the supreme Possibility.

But if we believe only in our little Mississippi or our little Potomac, it is clearly hopeless. And we do indeed believe passionately, millennially in the virtue of our old ways. They also hold an immense power – that of habit. It is remarkable, for they seem as solid as concrete, as convincing as all the old reasons of the world, the old habits of flowing in one direction or another, as irrefutable as Newton's apple, and yet, for the eye beginning to lose its scales, as unsubstantial as a cloud – one blows on them and they fall away. This is the mental Illusion, the formidable illusion that is blinding us.

* *
*

For the seeker, the illusion is demystified in small doses, in elusive but recurring little touches, through tiny little experiences that prompt him to open one eye and try, after all. But he must try very often before finding the lever, make endless mistakes, follow the old erroneous ways to unmask their false power. As always, this takes place in the microscopic commonplaceness of life. And he discovers the power of thought. Or rather, he discovers the energy value of a passing and apparently futile little thought that enters him naturally, "by chance."

He is clear, centered in his fire, carried by his cadence; then, out of habit, he starts the machinery up again. He fixes his look on this or that, lets a whole series of waves trigger old reflexes, open this valve, press that button, stir up a whole network in a second, which starts vibrating by degrees, awakening a reaction here, a desire there, a fear a little farther—the old circuit is reactivated. He meets again an old apprehension, an anxiety, a fear, a baseless defeatism. Actually, it really looks like a circuit of pain. And if he happens to look at that microscopic catastrophe (which is nothing, a passing breath), if he adds to it the weight of a reflection (not even a reflection, just a lingering look), the small commotion soon begins to blow up, to stick and settle in for good—it looks like a tiny little bubble of living power, no bigger than a fly, but so sticky. And the most remarkable thing is that it has its own independent force of propulsion: it goes to its goal obstinately, mechanically, automatically. Two days or two hours or two minutes later, under the surprised eyes of the seeker, who has remained clear enough to follow

the whole movement in detail, the results of his apprehension or desire or futile thought appear: "by accident," he twists his ankle, bumps into an old acquain-
tance, receives bad news, enters the confusion he had
foreseen. Everything is in league, conspires to go in the
wrong direction, converges on that little black or gray
bubble, as if it had attracted the circumstances and
events exactly in conformance, sympathetic we could
say, with the quality of vibration it emanates. It is a quasi-
instantaneous chemical reaction: this drop of litmus solution will turn everything red or blue or black. This is exactly the reverse process of the "correct thought" that
engenders the favorable circumstance. It looks almost
like a microscopic magic.

Indeed, it is magic. The seeker repeats the same experience ten, a hundred, times. And he begins to stare in
fascination. He begins, through a tiny experience, to ask
himself a stupendous why? . . . Oh, the world's secrets
are not concealed in thunder and flames! They are here,
just waiting for a consenting look, a simple way of being
that does not constantly put up its habitual barriers, its
possibles or impossibles, its you-can'ts and you-mustn'ts,
its buts and more buts, its ineluctables, and the whole
train of its iron laws, the old laws of an animal-man who
goes round and round in the cage built with his own
hands. He looks about himself, and the experience multi-
plies, as if it were thrust before his very eyes, as if that
simple little effort for truth sparked innumerable answers, precipitated circumstances, encounters, demonstrations, as if it were saying, "Look, look, this is how it
works." A consciousness beyond words lays its finger of
light upon each encounter. The true picture emerges
from behind appearances. A breath of truth here elicits
the same truth in each thing and each movement. And he
sees. . . . He does not see miracles—or rather, he sees

sordid little miracles blindly contrived by blind magicians. He sees poor humans in droves weaving the pretty bubble, patiently and tirelessly inflating it, each day adding their little breath of defeat or desire or helplessness, their miasma of self-doubt, their little noxious thoughts, stretching and nurturing the iridescent bubble of their knowledge and petty triumphs, the implacable bubble of their science, the bubble of their charity or virtue. And they go on, prisoners of a bubble, entangled in the network of force they have carefully woven, accumulated, piled up day after day. Each act results from that thrust; each circumstance is the obscure gravitation of that attraction, and everything moves mechanically, ineluctably, mathematically as we have willed it in a black or yellow or decrepit little bubble. And the more we kick and strain and struggle and draw this force inside to break the pretty or not so pretty wall, the harder it becomes, as if our ultimate effort still brought to it an ultimate strength. And we say we are the victims of circumstances, victims of this or that; we say we are poor, sick, ill-fated; we say we are rich, virtuous, triumphant. We say we are thousands of things under thousands of colors and bubbles, and there is nothing of the kind, no rich, no poor, no sick, no virtuous or victim; there is something else, oh, radically different, which is awaiting its hour. There is a secret godhead smiling.

And the bubble grows. It takes in families, peoples, continents; it takes in every color, every wisdom, every truth, and envelops them. There is that breath of light, that note of beauty, the miracle of those few lines caught in architecture or geometry, that instant of truth that heals and delivers, that lovely curve glimpsed in a flash which links that star to this destiny, this asymptote to that hyperbola, this man to that song, this gesture to that effect – and more men come, men by the thousands, who come puffing and inflating the little bubble, creating pink and blue and everlasting religions, infallible salvations in the great bubble, summits of light that are the sum of their compounded little hopes, abysses of hell that are the sum of their cherished fears; who come adding this note and that idea, this grain of knowledge and that healing second, this conjunction and that curve, that moment of effectiveness beneath the dust of the myriads of galaxies, and erecting their black temples, yellow temples, polychromatic temples, devising unquestionable medicines under the great bubble, irreducible sciences, implacable geometries, charts of illness, charts of recovery, charts of destiny. And everything twists and turns as the doctor willed it under the great fateful Bubble, as the scientist willed it, as that moment of coincidence among the countless myriads of lines in the universe has decided it for the eternity of time. We have seized a minute of the world and made it into a sublime law. We have seized a spark and made it into the huge amber light that blinds and suffocates us in the great mental bubble. And there is nothing of the kind – not one single law, not one single illness, not one single medical or scientific dogma, not one single temple is true, not one perpetual chart, not one single destiny under the stars – there is a tremendous mental hypnotism, and behind, far, far behind, and yet right here, so much here, immediately here, something impregnable, unseizable by any snare, unrestricted by any law, invulnerable to every illness and every hypnotism, unsaved by our salvations, unsullied by our sins, unsullied by our virtues, free from every destiny and every chart, from every golden or black bubble – a pure, infallible bird that can recreate the world in the twinkling of an eye. We change our look, and everything changes. Gone is the pretty bubble. It is here – if we want.

*
* *

When the bubble bursts, we begin to enter supermanhood. We begin to enter Harmony. Oh, it does not
burst through our efforts; it does not give way through
any amount of virtues and meditation, which on the contrary further harden the bubble, give it such a lovely
shine, such a captivating light that it indeed takes us captive, and we are all the more prisoners as the more
beautiful the bubble is, held more captive by our good
than by our evil—there is nothing harder in the world
then a truth caught in a trap; it turns the trap into a hard
paradise. But Truth, the Great Truth, the beautiful Harmony is not caught in our traps; it does not care at all
about our virtues and accumulated merits, our brilliant
talents or even our obscure weaknesses. Who is great?
Who is small and obscure, or less obscure, beneath the
drifting of the galaxies that look like the dust of a great
Sun? The Truth, the ineffable Sweetness of things and of
each thing, the living Heart of millions of beings who do
not know, does not require us to become true to bestow
its truth upon us—who could become true, who could become other than he is, what are we actually capable of?
We are capable of pain and misery aplenty; we are capable of smallness and more smallness, error garbed in a
speck of light, knowledge that stumbles into its own
quagmires, a good that is the luminous shadow of its secret evil, freedom that imprisons itself in its own salvation—we are capable of suffering and suffering, and even
our suffering is a secret delight. The Truth, the light
Truth, escapes our dark or luminous snares. It runs,
breathes with the wind, cascades with the spring, cascades everywhere, for it is the spring of everything. It
even murmurs in the depths of our falsehood, winks an
eye in our darkness and pokes fun at us. It sets its light
traps for us, so light we do not see them; it beckons us in
a thousand ways at every instant and everywhere, but it

is so fleeting, so unexpected, so contrary to our habitual way of looking at things, so unserious that we walk right past it. We cannot make head or tail out of it; or else we stick a beautiful label on it to trap it in our magic. And it still laughs. It plays along with our magic, plays along with our suffering and geometry; it plays the millipede and the statistician; it plays everything – it plays whatever we want. Then, one day, we no longer really want; we no longer want any of all that, neither our gilded miseries, nor our captivating lights nor our good nor our evil, nor any of that whole polychromatic array in which each color changes into the other: hope into despair, effort into backlash, heaven into prison, summit into abyss, love into hate, and each wrested victory into a new defeat, as if each plus attracted its minus, each for its against, and everything forever went forward, backward, right and left, bumping into the wall of the same prison, white or black, green or brown, golden or less golden. We no longer want any of all that; we are only that cry of need in our depths, that call for air, that fire for nothing, that useless little flame that goes along with our every step, walks with our sorrows, walks and walks night and day, in good and evil, in the high and the low and everywhere. And this fire soon becomes like our drop of good in evil, our bit of treasure in misery, our glimmer of light in the chaos, all that remains of a thousand gestures and passing lights, the little nothing that is like everything, the tiny song of a great ongoing misery – we no longer have any good or evil, any high or low, any light or darkness, any tomorrow or yesterday. It is all the same, miserable in black and white, but we have that abiding little fire, that tomorrow of today, that murmur of sweetness in the depths of pain, that virtue of our sin, that warm drop of being in the high and the low, day and night, in shame and in joy, in solitude and in the crowd, in approval and disapproval—it is all the same. It burns and burns. It is tomorrow, yesterday, now and forever. It is our one song of being, our little note of fire, our paradise in a little flame, our freedom in a little flame, our knowledge in a little flame, our summit of flame in a void of being, our vastness in a tiny singing flame—we know not why. It is our companion, our friend, our wife, our bearer, our country—it *is*. And it feels good. Then, one day, we raise our head, and there is no more bubble. There is that Fire burning softly everywhere, recognizing all, loving all, understanding all, and it is like a heaven without trouble; it is so simple that we never thought of it, so tranquil that each drop is like an ocean, so smiling and clear that it goes through everything, enters and slips in everywhere—it plays here, plays there, as transparent as air, a nothing that changes everything; and perhaps it is everything.

We are in the Harmony of the new world.

Some poets and sages have touched this Harmony, some rare musicians have heard it and attempted to translate a few notes of that singing vastness. It flows on high, on the summits of consciousness, an endless rhythm without high or low, through blue eternities, flowing and flowing like a joy that would sing itself, rolling its immense flood over eternal hills, carrying those heavenly bodies and all those earths and seas, carrying everything in its blazing and tranquil surge—an unutterable sound that would contain all sounds and all notes in one, a fusion of music, a golden outburst one single time of a cry of love or a cry of joy issuing from the abyss of time; a pure triumph that has seen all those worlds and ages in a glance, and the sorrow of a child on the bank of that blue river and the softness of the paddy fields and the death of that old man, the tiny tranquillity of a leaf quivering in the south wind, and others, countless others that are always the same, that go up and down the great river, cross here or there, pass without ever passing, grow up and disappear in the distance, into a great golden sea whence they came, carried by a little rhythm of the great rhythm, a little spark of the great undying golden fire, a persisting little note that pervades all lives, all deaths, all sorrows and joys; an ineffable blue expansion of space that fills the lungs with a sort of eternal air, a sort of resurrection; a bursting out of music everywhere as if space were nothing but music, nothing but singing azure—a powerful, triumphant flowing that carries us on forever, as if wrapped in its wings of glory. And all is fulfilled. The universe is a miracle.

But the earth, the little earth, reels below, reels in its pain. It does not know or see the joy upholding it, and which it is—for how could anything be without that joy which holds everything, that persistent memory of joy which pulls at the heart of things and beings?

I, Earth, have a deeper power than Heaven;
 My lonely sorrow surpasses its rose-joys,
A red and bitter seed of the raptures seven;—
 My dumbness fills with echoes of a far Voice.

By me the last finite, yearning, strives
 To reach the last infinity's unknown,
The Eternal is broken into fleeting lives
 And Godhead pent in the mire and the stone. [24]

And the Rhythm, the great Rhythm, was scattered, broken up, pulverized to enter the heart of its world and make itself the size of the millipede or a little leaf quivering in the wind, to make itself understood by a brain, loved by a passerby. We have drawn from it syncopated music, multicolored pictures, joys, sorrows, since we could no longer contain its whole, unbroken flow. We have made it into equations, poems, architecture; we have trapped it in our machines, locked it in an amulet or a thought, since we could no longer bear the pressure of its great direct flow. And we have made dungeons, hells, which were the absence of that rhythm, the lack of a lungful of eternal air, the suffocation of a little man who believes only in his suffering, only in the push buttons of his machine and the walls of his intelligence. We have graphed, multiplied, broken down, atomized to infinity; and we could no longer make out or understand anything, since we had lost the one little breath of the great breath, the one little sign of the great Direction, the little note that loves and understands all. And since we had closed everything around us, locked ourselves in a shell, armor-plated ourselves in our thinking logic, equipped ourselves with irrefutable helmets and antennas, we have declared that that Harmony, that Rhythm, did not exist, that it was far, far above, the paradise of our virtues, the crackling of our little antennas, the dream of a collective unconscious, the product of the evolved earthworm, the meeting of two enamored molecules—like the savage of old who used to cut up the unknown lands, we have cut up space and time, thrown back into another geography the Ganges and El Dorados we have not yet crossed, the pretty fords of that little river. But that Ganges and that El Dorado are here, as well as many other marvels, many other currents of the great Current. All is here, under our feet, if we will only open the little shell and stop putting off until heaven or doomsday what sings in each minute of time and each pebble of space.

This is the Harmony of the new world, the joy of the greater Self. It is here, instantly, if we want. All it takes is removing our blinders. All it takes is a true look, a simple look at the great world. All it takes is a little fire inside to consume all the shells and sufferings and bubbles—for the only suffering is to be confined there.

11

The Change of Power

BUT, in truth, this Harmony of the new world is not expressed by great music or ecstatic joys. It is far more discreet and far more efficient – maybe we should say far more demanding.

There is but one Harmony, as there is one Consciousness and one earthly body, which are those of the greater Self, but this Harmony and Consciousness are unveiled a little at a time, as we grow and the scales fall from our eyes, and their effects are different, depending at what level we grasp them. Harmony chants high above, and it is grand and sublime, but it has chanted for millenia and ages without changing much in the world and the hearts of men. And evolution has rolled its cycles, descending, it seems, into an altogether material grossness, density and ignorance, a darkness adorned with all the artifices of the gods to make us believe that we were the masters, while we were really the servants of a machinery, the slaves of a small loose bolt which was enough to blow up the beautiful machine and expose the old untouched savage underneath. Indeed that evolution has descended; it has cast us down from our fragile heights and golden ages, which were perhaps not so golden as it is said, to force us to find here, too, that Light and Harmony and Consciousness, in this low place, which is low only for us. In fact, there is no descent, no fall, no move backward; there is a never-ending precipitation of truth and harmony, which touches deeper and deeper layers to reveal to them the light and joy they always were—had we not fallen, the light would never have penetrated our hovel, matter would never have gotten out of its night. Each descent is an opening of light, each fall, a new degree of blossoming. Through our evil the substance is transmuted. And our evil is perhaps quite simply the unknown territory we wrest from its "nonexistence," the way Columbus's sailors wrested the perilous Indies from their "night."

But the passage is perilous.

In fact, the first effect of Truth as it touches a new layer is to produce a frightful disorder, or so it seems. The first effects of mental truth when it touched the primates must have been traumatic, we can assume, and utterly subversive of the simian order and effectiveness; a peasant has only to take a book for the first time for all his bucolic peace to be upset and his sound and simple notion of things to be thrown into turmoil. Truth is a great disturber. Indeed if it were not there to goad and press on the world, the stone would have forever remained in its mineral bliss and man in his satisfied economy—which is why no supereconomy, no acme of political ingenuity, no perfection of egalitarianism or distribution of human wealth, nor even any paroxysm of charity and philanthropy can ever satisfy the heart of man and halt the irresistible onrush of Truth. Truth can only stop at the totality of Truth—the totality of Joy and Harmony in each particle and the entire universe—although it will not stop anywhere, for Truth is infinite and its marvels inexhaustible. We tend quite naturally and anthropocentrically to declare that we make great efforts to attain light and truth, and this and that, but it may be presumptuousness on our part, and the lotus seed rises inevitably toward the light, wrenches itself free from the mud and bursts open in the sunshine, in spite of all its efforts to become, say, a water lily or a supertulip—and that Sun presses and presses, churns and kneads and ferments its rebellious soil, brings its chemical ingredients to a boil and breaks the husk, till everything is returned to its ultimate beauty, in spite of all our efforts to become, say, just a social and intelligent fellow. The great Sun of evolution presses upon its world, cracking its old molds, fermenting the heresies of the future and bringing to a boil the pale canned wisdoms of the mental legislators. Was there ever a more desperate time, more empty, more dreadfully confined in its flimsy triumphs and enameled virtues than the so-called *belle époque?* But that enamel is cracking, and so much the better; the beautiful machine is cracking, and so much the better; all our virtues and mental certainties and fantasies of a great economic Disneyland on earth are crumbling, and again, so much the better. Truth, the great Harmony to be, is mercilessly tightening its screw on our intellectual helmets, exposing each speck of dirt, each weakness, drawing out the poison and churning its humanity, like the "ocean of unconsciousness" of the Puranic legends, until it yields all its nectar of immortality.

And the seeker discovers—on his own small scale, in the microcosm he represents—that the Harmony of the new world, the new consciousness he has touched gropingly, is a tremendous transforming Power. In the past, it may have chanted up above, produced lovely poems and cathedrals of wisdom and beauty, but when it touches matter, it takes on the austere face of the angry Mother, thrashing her children and sculpting them mercilessly into the image of her own demanding Rectitude – and compassion, the infinite grace that stops just in time, administers just the necessary dose and does not inflict one ounce of suffering more than is indispensable. When the seeker begins to open his eyes to this Compassion, this infinite wisdom in the minutest detail, these unbelievable detours to achieve a fuller and more encompassing perfection, these studied obscurities and concerted rebellions, these falls into a greater light, and the infinite march of a Beauty that leaves no hidden stain, no trace of imperfection, no refuge of weakness or disguised pettiness, no recess of falsehood, he is filled with a wonder that surpasses all sidereal measures and cosmic magic. For, truly, being able to attend to such a microscopic point of matter – so futile under the stars, so complicated in its tangle of pain and revolt, its obscure resistance that threatens disaster at every instant, and those thousands of little disasters to ward off every day and at every step, those millions of little sufferings to transmute without blowing up the world – requires a power such as the earth has never known before. Disease is breaking out everywhere, in every country, every consciousness, every atom of the great earthly body – this is a merciless revolution, a relentless transmutation – and yet, here and there, in each human consciousness, each country, each fragment of the great torn body, the catastrophe is avoided at the last minute, the best slowly comes out of the worst, consciousness awakens, and our stumbling steps take us despite themselves to the ultimate gate of deliverance. Such is the formidable Harmony, the imperative Power that the seeker discovers step by step and in his own substance.

We have therefore come to a new change of power. A new power such as there has never been since the first anthropoids, a tidal wave of power that has nothing to do with our little philosophical and spiritual meditations of past ages, a worldwide, collective and perhaps universal phenomenon as radically new as the first surge of thought upon the world, when mind took over from the simian order and overthrew all its laws and instinctual mechanisms. But here—and this is really the characteristic of the new world being born—the power is not a power of abstraction, not a talent for getting a bird's-eye view of things and reducing the scattered data of the world into an equation in order to make a synthesis, which is always wobbly—the mind has turned everything into abstraction; it lives in an image of the world, a yellow or blue reflection of the great bubble, like a man inside a glass statue—not a discursive and contingent power that only adds and subtracts, not a gathering of knowledge that never makes a whole. It is a direct power of the truth of each instant and each thing harmonized with the total truth of the millions of instants and things, a "power to enter" the truth of each gesture and each circumstance, which accords with all other gestures and circumstances because Truth is *one* and the Self is unique, and if this point is touched, everything else is instantly touched, like cell and cell of the same body. It is a tremendous power of concretization of Truth, acting directly upon the same Truth contained in each point of space and each second of time, or rather, compelling each moment, each circumstance, each gesture, each cell of matter to yield its truth, its right note, its own innate power buried under all the layers of our vital and mental accretions—a tremendous truing of the world and each being. We could say a tremendous Movement of "realization"—the world is not real! It is a distorted appearance, a mental approximation, which looks more like a nightmare, a black and white translation of something we still have not seized. We do not have our real eyes yet! For, in the end, there is only one reality, and that is the reality of Truth—a truth that has grown, that had to protect itself behind walls, to limit and dim itself under one shell or another, one bubble or another, to make itself felt by a caterpillar or a man, then bursts open in its own Sunlight when the wings of the great Self we always were begin to open.

But this change of power, this transition from the indirect and abstract truths of the mind to the direct and concrete Truth of the great Self is obviously not effected on the summits of the Spirit—it has nothing to do with mental gymnastics, just as the other power had nothing to do with the ape's skills. It is effected in a most down-to-earth way, in everyday life, in the minuscule, the futility of the moment, which is futile only to us, if we understand that a speck of dust contains as much truth as the totality of all space, and just as much power. It therefore applies itself to utterly material mechanisms. The play takes place in the substance. Therefore it comes up against age-old resistances, against a bubble that is perhaps the first self-defensive bubble of the protoplasm in its water hole. But in the end "resistances turn out to have assisted by the resistance much more than they have impeded the intention of the great Creatix and her Mover,"[25] and we do not know, finally, if there is a single resistance, a single microscopic defense, a single play of shadow and pain that does not secretly build up the very power we are trying to manifest. If it emerged too soon, truth would be incomplete, or unbearable for the other animalcules that share our water hole and which would soon disgorge it—we are a single human body, we always forget, and our mistakes or slowness are the mistakes and slowness of the world. But if we can win a victory here, in this little point of matter, we will win it in all the points of the world. For, actually, each of us human beings has a formidable task to carry out, if he understands.

Being born in this world is a far more powerful mystery than we had thought.

*
* *

For a long time now the seeker has got rid of the mental machinery. He has also brought order to the vital machinery. And if old desires, wills or reactions still come to muddy his clearing, they are rather on the order of a motion-picture image projected onto a screen, out of habit, but without real substance. The seeker has lost the habit of sitting in the screen and identifying with the characters – he looks; he is clear; he observes everything; he is centered in his fire which dissipates all those clouds. From then on, another level of entanglement comes more and more to light, another degree of the machine (this is truly a "path of descent"): a material, subconscious mechanism. But so long as he is not clear, he sees nothing; he cannot unravel those threads which are so intertwined with his habitual activities, and "mentalized" like all the rest, that they make up an altogether natural web. This material, subconscious mechanism then becomes extremely concrete, like the whirlings of the goldfish in its glass bowl. But let us emphasize that this is not the subconscious small fry of the psychoanalysts – those fry belong to the mental bubble; they are merely the reverse of the little surface fellow, the action of his reactions, the knot of his desires, the constriction of his nurtured smallness, the past of his old little story inside a bubble, the goat tether of his small separate ego tied to the social and familial and religious stake, and the countless stakes that tie men inside a bubble. And we strongly suspect that those dreamers simply go on dreaming inside a psychoanalytical bubble, the way others dream inside a religious one of hells and paradises that exist only in man's mental imagination. But, as long as one is inside the bubble, it is implacable and irrefutable; its hells are real hells, its filth real filth, and one is the prisoner of a little bright or dark cloud. So let us say, in passing, that one does not free oneself from the mud by digging in the mud and unwholesomely plowing up the byways of the frontal fellow (one might as well take a bath in dirty water to get clean), one does not free oneself from the bubble by the lights of the bubble, or from evil by a good that is only its reverse, but by a something else that is not of the bubble: a very simple little fire within and everywhere, which is the key to freedom, all freedoms, and to the world.

This subconscious resistance is very difficult to describe. It has a thousand faces, as many as there are individuals, and for each the color is different, the "syndrome," so to say, is different. Each one of us has his particular "drama," with its staging, preferred situations, puppetry or Grand Guignol. But it is one and the same puppet show under all colors, one and the same story behind all the words – and the same resistance everywhere. It is *the* resistance, the point that says no. It does not reveal itself immediately; it is elusive, cunning. In fact, we really believe it loves drama. It is its raison d'être and the salt of its life, and, if it no longer had any drama to grind out, it would make up some – it is the dramatist par excellence. It is perhaps even the great dramatist of all this chaotic and painful life that we see. But each of us harbors his little man of the big "man of sorrow,"[26] as Sri Aurobindo used to call him. The drama of the world will stop when we begin to put a stop to our own little drama. But the clever puppet slips between our fingers. Driven off the mental stage where it ran its explanatory and questioning machinery – it is a tireless questioner; it asks questions for the pleasure of asking, and if all its questions were answered, it would come up with more, for it is also a great doubter—ousted from the mind, it sinks down one degree further to play its number on the vital stage. There it is on more solid ground. (The further it descends, the stronger it becomes, and all the way down at the bottom, it is the very image of strength, the knot par excellence, the irreducible point, the absolute NO.) We are all more or less familiar with its tricks on the vital stage: its great game of passion and desire, sympathy and antipathy, hate and love—but in fact they are the two faces of the same food, and it savors evil as much as good, suffering as much as joy; it is just a way of swallowing in one direction or another. Even charity and philanthropy serve its purpose. It grows fatter either way. The more virtuous it is, the harder it is. Idealism and patriotism, sacred or less sacred causes are its clever victuals. It has mastered the art of dressing itself in superb motives; it can be found at the parties of charity volunteers and Peace conferences—but of course Peace never comes, for if by some miracle Peace ever came, or the eradication of all poverty on earth, what would it do for a living? Driven off that stage, it sinks one degree lower and disappears into the dungeons of the subconscious. Not for long. There it begins to become clear, so to say, and show its real face. It has grown very small, very hard, a sort of grinning caricature: "the grisly Elf," as Sri Aurobindo calls it.

> *[Man] harbours within him a grisly Elf*
> *Enamoured of sorrow and sin.*
> *The grey Elf shudders from heaven's flame*
> *And from all things glad and pure;*
> *Only by pleasure and passion and pain*
> *His drama can endure.* [27]

It is ready for anything, latches onto anything, takes advantage of the least crack to force its way back on stage, the slightest pretext to spit out its inky cloud and overcast everything in an instant. A thick, black and sticky instant cloud. It is a fight to the death, for it knows perfectly well it is going to die. It is its last hand, the very one now playing its last card in the world. At the bottom, all the way down at the very bottom, it is a microscopic knot of pain, something that shrinks from the sun and joy, something suffocating and frightened of vastness. It is as hard as rock, perhaps as hard as the original rock of the earth. A dark NO to life and NO to everything. It simply will *not*. It is there, and it will not budge. It is perhaps the essence of death, the root of night, the original cry of the earth spurred by the Sun of Truth.

And it remains there to the end—in fact, the end of the end—it remains there perhaps to force us to descend to rock bottom and discover our immortal face beneath this mask of death. If it were not there, we might all have already fled into the heavens of the Spirit. But it is said that our immortality and our heaven must be wrought in matter and through our body.

If we can catch that painful elf—for it is pain itself—just before it buries itself completely, it exhibits a whole daily, material and imperceptible mechanism. This is the great resistance to the change of power, the molehill trying to stay the law of Harmony. Therefore it is where the battle is taking place at this moment, in the microcosm and the macrocosm. It is like a caricature (or the more exact face) of all the polished and civilized activities of the brilliant elf of the higher levels: doubt, fear, avidity, self-centeredness, all the contractions, prehensions and apprehensions of the mental pseudopod. It is a minuscule and ridiculous functioning, and, if by chance we notice it, we shrug it off or attach no importance to it. But we are wrong. We look at everything from atop our mental arrogance, as if those trifles were inconsequential. But they have staggering consequences. We do not see it because we live in our logical and symmetrical clouds. But life grates; there is an immense, universal grating whose source lies in those ridiculous little grains of sand. At the level of matter, there are no "little things," because everything is made of little things, and that absurd reaction of doubt or fear is the incalculable equivalent of the mental misjudgment that makes us shut the door on a brilliant opportunity. We are constantly shutting the door on Harmony, turning our backs on the miracle, locking out possibilities, and making ourselves sick into the bargain. For, at the material level, this Harmony does not flow in majestic symphonies through the great arteries of the spirit; it uses what it has. It percolates through minuscule channels, fragile filaments quivering within our material consciousness; it enters in droplets, spurts, discrete quanta that look like nothing – a passing breath, a flicker of a smile, a wave of ease without reason – which change everything. We do not notice the change because we live in our normal chaos, our usual suffocation, but the seeker, who has become a little clearer, begins to notice, to sense those minute changes of density, those sudden obstructions, those minuscule expansions, those air pockets in his material substance. He sees the almost instant effect of a tiny little emanation of doubt, an absurd fear or tensing up without apparent cause, a ridiculous and morbid imagination crossing his atmosphere. He discovers a thousand sly little pulsations, deceitful palpitations, dark impulses in the great material pond. He puts his finger on fear, the great, voracious and retractile Fear which covers the world like the protoplasm inside its gelatine membrane – the slightest touch, the least breath of air, the tiniest ray of sun, and it contracts, shuts the door and rolls up into a ball in its membrane. The immediate reaction to everything is NO; then, sometimes, a yes blurted out, as if impelled by the same fear of missing something. He discovers the fantastic morbid and defeatist imagination of matter, as if, for matter, life represented a kind of dreadful invasion from which it had never quite recovered, a fall perhaps from the original bliss of the stone, an irruption of death into its peaceful routine. Everything is liable to bring catastrophe – the great catastrophe of Life – expectation of the worst, anticipation of the worst, almost a wish and call for the worst, so this tragedy of life may be stopped at last and everything return to the peace and beatific immobility of dust. He discovers how diseases break out, matter decays, substance ages – the great difficulty of living, the contraction onto self, the suffocation inside, the hardening of all the little arteries through which a drop of all-curing harmony might have seeped in. He hears his fill of petty whining, small grudges, matter's wounded negations, and above all – above all – its despairing leitmotif: "This is impossible, that is impossible. . . ." For matter, everything is "impossible," because the only sure possibility is the inviolable immobility of the stone. Because all movement of life and hope is still a stirring of death. And it shuts the door, turns off the light, refuses the miracle – we *all* refuse the miracle. We are firmly seated atop our cancer, the doubters of the great immortal Harmony, the dwarves of the earth who believe in pain, believe in disease, believe in suffering, believe in death: This is impossible, impossible, impossible. . . .

So the seeker learns the lesson of Harmony. He learns it step by step, by trial and error, tiny little errors that sow disease and confusion. At this stage, the experience no longer takes place in the intellect or heart; it takes place in the body. There is a minute play of sensations, as fleeting as must have been the first quiver of the radiolarian under the temperature changes in the Gulf Stream, and as laden with physical consequences as a storm over the lovely wheat fields of the mind or a typhoon over the murky seas of the vital. We are so dense and blind on our "higher" levels that we need to be hit over the head to understand that the man in front of us is angry and that murder is lurking in those eyes so transparent. But matter is refined; the more we experience it, the more we discover its incredible receptivity, working in both directions, alas. A hundred times or a thousand times, the seeker is confronted with those microtyphoons, those minute whirlwinds that abruptly overturn the whole equilibrium of the being, becloud everything, give a taste of ashes and despair to the slightest gesture, decompose the air he breathes and decompose everything – an instantaneous general decomposition for one second, ten seconds. A hardening of everything. The seeker is suddenly overwhelmed with fatigue; he sees illness coming – and it is indeed coming straight at him. Which illness? *The* Illness. And just behind, lying in wait, death. In one second, ten seconds, one goes straight to the point; one touches the thing. It is right there, irrefutable: the whole mechanism out in the open, like a sudden call of death. Yet, outside, everything is the same. The circumstances are the same, the gestures the same; the sun still shines and the body comes and goes as usual. But everything is changed. It is a flash-death, an instantaneous cholera. Then it vanishes, dissipates like a cloud, one hardly knows why. But if one gives in, one truly falls ill, breaks a leg or has a real accident. And the seeker starts learning the reason for those minuscule reversals of equilibrium. He tracks down a minuscule hell, which is perhaps the first seed of the great million-faced Evil, the first hardening of death's great blissful petrification. Everything is contained there, in a black spark. But the day we catch hold of that tiny poisonous vibration, we will have the secret of immortality, or at least that of the prolongation of life at will. We die because we give in, and we give in in thousands of little instances. The choice between death and immortality must be made again at every instant.

But this is still a negative and human way of approaching the experience. In fact, the Harmony, the marvelous Harmony that attends to everything, does not want to teach us the laws of hell, even a minute hell. It wants the sunlit law. It flings its typhoons and illnesses at us, casts us down into the black pit, only as much as is necessary for us to learn the lesson, not one minute more. And the second we have recaptured the speck of sun, the little note, the miraculous and tranquil little flowing in the heart of things, everything changes, is cured, tilts into the light – an instantaneous miracle. Actually, it is not a miracle. The miracle is everywhere, at each instant; it is the very nature of the universe, its air, its sun, its breathing of harmony. Only we keep blocking the way, putting up our walls, our sciences, our millions of devices that "know better" than this Harmony. We must learn to let it flow freely, to let go – there is no other secret. It does not "push us down" to crush us or punish us, but to teach us the technique of mastery. It wants us to be the true masters of its solar Secret, to be fully what we have always been, free and kings and joyous, and it will pound and pound our miserable secrets until we are forced to knock at its sunlit door, to open our hands and let its sweetness flow over the world and into our hearts.

For there is an even greater Secret. We face this enormous universe bristling with difficulties and problems and negations and obstacles – everything is a sort of constant impossibility to be overcome by dint of intelligence, will-power, material or spiritual muscles. But, by so doing, we are on equal terms with the caterpillar, on equal terms with the fear-stricken gnome in its death hole. And, because we believe in difficulty, we are compelled to believe in our muscles of steel or not—which always collapse. And we believe in death, we believe in evil, we believe in suffering, as the mole believes in the virtues of its tunnels. But by our morbid belief, our age-old belief, our gray-elf look, we have hardened the difficulty, armed it with a host of instruments and remedies that inflated it even more, planted it more firmly in its implacable groove. The world is enveloped in a formidable elfin illusion. It is in the grip of a formidable Death, which is but our fear of immortality. It is being torn apart by a formidable suffering, which is our refusal of joy and sunshine. Yet everything is here, every possible miracle, in the great open sunlight, every dreamed and undreamed possibility, every simple, spontaneous and natural mastery, every simple power of the Great Harmony. It asks only to pour over the world, flow through our channels and our bodies. All it asks is that we open the passageway. If we let that lightness, that divine ease, that solar smile, flood for a second our little aggregate of flesh, everything melts, obstacles dissolve, illnesses vanish, circumstances are straightened out as if by miracle, the darkness is illumined, the wall collapses—as though they had never existed. And once again, it is not even a miracle; it is simplicity reestablished, reality restored. It is the point of harmony here contacting Harmony everywhere and spontaneously, automatically, instantly bringing (or restoring) harmony there, in that gesture, that circumstance, that word, that particular conjunction of events—and everything is a marvel of conjunction because everything flows from the Law. The walls never were; the obstacles never were; evil, suffering and death never were. But we had that look of evil, that look of suffering and death, that look of the imprisoned elf. The world is as we see it, as we want it. There is another Look within us which can transfigure everything. "My children," said She who continued Sri Aurobindo's work, "you all live in an enormous sea of vibrations and you don't even realize it! Because you are not receptive. There is such a resistance in you that if something manages to penetrate, three quarters of what enters is violently thrown out because of an incapacity to contain it.... Take simply the example of the consciousness of Forces, such as the force of love, the force of comprehension, the force of creation (it is the same for all of them: the force of protection, the force of growth, the force of progress, all of them), just take Consciousness, the consciousness that covers everything, permeates everything, that is everywhere and in everything—it is almost felt as something trying to impose itself violently on the being, which balks!... Whereas if you were open and simply breathed—that's all, just breathed—you would breathe in Consciousness, Light, Comprehension, Force, Love and all the rest."[28] Everything is there under our eyes, the total marvel of the world, just waiting for our consent, our look of faith in beauty, in freedom, in the supreme possibility that is knocking at our doors, pounding on the walls of our intelligence, suffering and pettiness. This is the supreme "change of power," which is knocking at the world's doors and hammering away at nations, churches and Sorbonnes, hammering at human consciousnesses and all our geometric and well-thought-out certainties. And if once, only once, man's consciousness opens up to one ray of that living miracle, if the consciousness of a single nation among all our blind nations opens up to one spark of that Grace, then this implacable civilization walled up in its science and laws, in an elf of terror and suffering – this enormous structure in which we have been born and which seems so inescapable, so indestructible and triumphant in its heavy miracles of steel and uranium, this clever prison in which we go in circles – will crumble as fast as it came into existence, leaving behind a pile of rust. Then we will be man at last, or superman rather. We will have joy, natural oneness, freedom without walls and power without tricks. Then we will realize that all this suffering, these walls and difficulties which besiege our life were only the spur of the Sun of Truth, an original restriction to increase our strength, our need for space and our power of truth, a veil of illusion to protect our eyes from too strong a light, a dark passage from the instinctive spontaneity of the animal to the conscious spontaneity of the superman – and that in the end everything is simple, unbelievably simple, like Truth itself, and unbelievably easy, like the very Joy that conceived these worlds. For, in truth, "the path of the gods is a sunlit path on which difficulties lose all reality."[29]

12

The Sociology of Superman

IN ITSELF, this change of power would not be enough to change the world if it were confined to only a few individuals. Actually, from the very beginning, from the very first steps, the seeker has realized that this yoga of the superman was not an individual yoga, though the individual is the starting point and instrument of the work, but a collective yoga, a form of concentrated evolution in which the individual is but an outpost, the spreader of the possibility, the embodier and transmitter of the new vibration. It is a yoga of the earth. What difference would a glorious superman make, sitting all alone on his vain throne of harmony? Although we suppose that the first primates which unknowingly did the yoga of the mind must not have been legion; and yet the mental possibility did spread from one to another. It was there, "in the air," pressing upon the old simian structures. Similarly, the superman possibility is there, in the air. Its time has come. It is liberally hammering at human consciousnesses and countries – men are unknowingly and unwittingly doing the yoga of the superman. This is not a theory we are advancing but an evolutionary fact, whether we like it or not. Only, the main difference between the premental era and ours is that human consciousnesses, however closed, stubborn, obscure and petty, have become capable of perceiving the direction of their own evolution and hence of accelerating and lending themselves to the process. That was the sole real purpose of the mental era: to lead us irresistibly to the point where we had to pass into something else, all together, by the very development of our consciousness and the very force that each of us and each country had accumulated in a little individual bubble. And the new level of integration will prove to us that the superman is not a denial of man but his fulfillment, not a denial of the mind but its rightful placement among the many tools, known and unknown, that man must use until the day he enters into possession of the direct power of Truth.

This understanding of the great Goal—or rather of the next goal, for the development is infinite—is one of the keys to collective realization. It takes only a little crack in the human consciousnesses, a tiny call for air, a very small prayer, one day, without reason, for the new Possibility to rush in and change our whole way of seeing and doing things. It does not expect great efforts or arduous discipline, as we have said; it awaits a moment of abandon, a tiny little cry inside, a little flame that awakens. And once men—a few men—have tasted that wine, they will never be able to go back to the old routine of suffering.

What, then, is the role of those who are beginning to understand and perhaps to experience? How does their work fit into the unconscious yoga of humanity? How can the movement spread and accelerate? What sort of collective realization can they bring into the world as a sample of what will be?

The first wave of this new consciousness is quite visible. It is perfectly chaotic. It has caught human beings unawares. Its ebb and flow can be seen everywhere: men have been seized with errantry, or aberrancy. They have set out in search of something they did not understand, but which pushed and prodded them inside; they have taken to the road to anywhere, knocked on every door, the good as well as the bad, broken through walls and windmills, or, suddenly seized with laughter, they have left bag and baggage and said goodbye to the old establishment. It is natural that the first reaction is aberrant, since by definition it leaves the old circuit, as the primate suddenly left the instinctive wisdom of the herd. Each transition to a higher equilibrium is at first a disequilibrium and total disruption of the old equilibrium. Therefore, these apprentice supermen, who do not even know each other, will more likely be found among the unorthodox elements of society, the so-called misfits, the bastards, the recalcitrants of the general prison, the rebels against they don't know what except they have had enough of it. They are the new crusaders without a crusade, the partisans without a party, the "antis" who are so much against that they no longer want any against or for; they want something else altogether, without plus or minus, offensive or defensive, without black, good, yes or no, something completely different and completely free from all the twists and turns of the Machine, which still would like to catch them in the nets of its negations as in the nets of its affirmations. Or else, at the opposite end of the spectrum, these apprentice supermen will perhaps be found among those who have traveled the long road of the mind, its labyrinths, its endless grind, its answers that answer nothing, that raise another question and still another, its solutions that solve nothing, and its whole painful round – its sudden futility at the end of the road, after a thousand questions and a thousand triumphs ever ruined, that little cry, at the end, of a man gaping at nothing and suddenly becoming like a helpless child again, as if all those days and years and labor had never been, as if nothing had happened, not a single real second in thirty years! These too, then, set out on the road. There, too, there is a crack for the Possible.

But the very conditions of the uprooting of the old order may for a long time falsify the quest for the new order. And at first, this new order does not exist; it has to be made. A whole world has to be invented. And the aspiring superman – or let us simply say the aspirant to "something else" – must confront a primary reality: the law of freedom is a very demanding one, infinitely more demanding than all the laws imposed by the Machine. It is not a coasting into just anything, but a methodical uprooting from thousands of little slaveries; it does not mean abandoning everything, but, on the contrary, taking charge of everything, since we no longer want to depend on anybody or anything. It is a supreme apprenticeship of responsibility – that of being oneself, which in the end is being all. It is not an escape, but a conquest; not a vacation from the Machine, but a great Adventure into man's unknown. And anything that may hamper this supreme freedom, at whatever level or under whatever appearance, must be fought as fiercely as the police or lawmakers of the old world. We are not leaving the slavery of the old order to fall into the worse slavery of ourselves – the slavery of drugs, of a party, of one religion or another, one sect or another, a golden bubble or a white one. We want the one freedom of smiling at everything and being light everywhere, identical in destitution and pomp, in prison and palace, in emptiness and fullness – and everything is full because we burn with the one little flame that possesses everything forever.

What will they do, these wanderers, these trans-humans of a new country that does not yet exist? In the first place, they will perhaps not move at all. They will perhaps have understood that the change has to be wrought inside and that,· if nothing changes inside, nothing will ever change outside for centuries and centuries. They will perhaps stay right where they are, in this little street, this gray country, in a humble disguise, an old routine, but it will no longer be a routine because they will do everything with another look, in another way, with another attitude – an inner way that changes all ways. And if they persevere, they will notice that this one little drop of true light they carry within themselves has the power to change everything about them surreptitiously. In their unpretentious little circle, they will have worked for the new world and precipitated a little more truth upon earth. But no circle is little when it has that center, since it is the center of everything. Or else, one day, perhaps they will feel impelled to join with their peers of the new world and with them build some living testimony of their common aspiration, as others built pyramids or cathedrals – perhaps a city of the new world. And this is the beginning of a great enterprise, and a great danger.

We have been so thoroughly mechanized, exteriorized, projected outside ourselves by our habit of depending on one mechanical device or another that our very first reflex is always to look for the external means, that is, an artifice, for all external means are artificial, part of the old falsehood. We will therefore be tempted to spread the idea, the Enterprise, through all the existing publicity channels, in short, to attract as many supporters of the new hope as possible – which will quickly become a new religion. Here it may be appropriate to quote Sri Aurobindo and to drive home positively and forcefully his categorical statement: "I don't believe in advertisement except for books etc., and in propaganda except for politics and patent medicines. But for serious work it is a poison. It means either a stunt or a boom—and stunts and booms exhaust the thing they carry on their crest and leave it lifeless and broken high and dry on the shores of nowhere—or it means a movement. A movement in the case of a work like mine means the founding of a school or a sect or some other damned nonsense. It means that hundreds or thousands of useless people join in and corrupt the work or reduce it to a pompous farce from which the Truth that was coming down recedes into secrecy or silence. It is what has happened to the 'religions' and is the reason of their failure."[30] True, ultimately all men, the entire earth belong to supermanhood, but the ABC's of the new consciousness, its governing principle, is diversity in Unity—and to try to confine the superman in advance to a ready-made setting, a privileged environment, an allegedly unique and more enlightened location is to fall back into the old farce and once again inflate the old human ego. To be sure, the law of Harmony will work in thousands of ways and in thousands of disguises, ultimately gathering the myriad notes of its great indivisible flow into a vaster space without boundaries. The Enterprise will be born everywhere at once—it is already born, whispering here and there, blindly banging against walls—and will gradually unveil its true face only when men are no longer able to trap it in a system, logic or shrine—when everything here below is a shrine, in every heart and every country. And men shall not even know how they were prepared for such a Marvel.

Those who know a little, who feel, who have begun to perceive the great Wave of Truth, will therefore not fall into the trap of "superman recruiting." The earth is unequally prepared; men are spiritually unequal despite all our democratic protests to the contrary—though they are essentially equal and vast in the great Self, and only one body with millions of faces – they have not all become the greatness that they are. They are on the way, and some dawdle while others seem to travel more swiftly, but the detours of the former are also part of the great geography of our indivisible domain, their delay or the brake they seem to apply to our motion is part of the fullness of perfection that we seek and which compels us to a greater meticulousness of truth. They too are going there, by their own way – and what is outside the way, in the end, since everything is the Way? He who knows a little, who feels, knows first and foremost, from having experienced it in his own flesh, that men are never truly brought together by artifices – and when they persist in their artifice, everything finally collapses and the "meeting" is brief; the beautiful school, the lovely sect, the little iridescent bubble of a moment's enthusiasm or faith is short-lived – they are brought together through a finer and more discreet law, a tiny little searchlight inside, twinkling and unassuming, but which sweeps across time and space, and touches a similar ray here and there, a twin frequency, a light source with the same intensity – and he goes. He goes haphazardly, takes a train, a plane, travels to this country and that one, believes he is searching for this or that, that he is in quest of adventure, the exotic, drugs or philosophy – he believes. He believes a lot of things. He thinks he has to have this power or that solution, this panacea or that revolution, this slogan or that one. He thinks he set out because of that thirst or revolt, that unhappy love affair or need for action, this hope or that old insoluble discord in his heart. But then, there is none of that! One day he stops, without knowing why, without planning to be there, without having looked for that place or that face, that insignificant village under the stars of one hemisphere or the other – and there it is. He has arrived. He has opened his one door, found his kindred fire, that look forever known; and he is exactly at the right place, at the right time, to do the right work. The world is a fabulous clockwork, if only we knew the secret of those little fires glowing in another space, dancing on a great inner sea where our skiffs sail as if guided by an invisible beacon.

*
* *

There are ten or twenty, perhaps fifty, here or there, in one latitude or another, who yearn to till a truer plot of land, a small patch of man to grow a truer being within themselves, perhaps create together a laboratory of the superman, lay the first stone of the City of Truth on earth. They do not know, they do not know anything, except that they need something else and that there exists a Law of Harmony, a marvelous "something" of the Future seeking to be incarnated. They want to find the conditions of that incarnation, to lend themselves to the trial, to offer their substance for that living experiment. They know nothing except that everything must be different: in hearts, in gestures, in matter and the handling of matter. They are not seeking to create a new civilization, but another man; not a supercity among the millions of buildings of the world, but a listening post for the forces of the future, a supreme yantra of Truth, a conduit, a channel to try to capture and inscribe in matter a first note of the great Harmony, a first tangible sign of the new world. They do not pose as the champions of anything; they do not defend any liberty or attack any ism. They simply try together. They are the champions of their own pure little note, which is unlike the next person's and yet is everyone's note. They are no longer from a country, a family, a religion or a party; they belong to their own party, which is no one else's and yet is the party of the world, because what becomes true at one point becomes true for the whole world and brings the whole world together. They are from a family to be invented, from a country yet to be born. They do not try to correct others or anybody, to pour self-glorifying charities over the world, to cure the poor and the lepers; they try to cure the great poverty of smallness in themselves, the gray elf of the inner misery, to reclaim one single parcel of truth from themselves, one single ray of harmony. For if that Disease is cured in our own heart or a few hearts, the world will be that much lighter, and, through our clarity, the Law of Truth will better penetrate matter and radiate all around spontaneously. What liberation, what relief can a man who suffers in his own heart bring to the world? They do not work for themselves, though they are the primary ground of the experience, but as an offering, pure and simple, to that which they do not really know, but which shimmers at the edge of the world like the dawn of a new age. They are the prospectors of the new cycle. They have given themselves to the future, body and soul, the way one jumps into the fire, without a look back. They are the servants of the infinite in the finite, of the totality in the infinitesimal, of eternity in each second and each gesture. They create their heaven with each step and carve the new world out of the banality of the day. And they are not afraid of failure, for they have left behind the failures and succes of the prison—they live in the sole infallibility of a right little note.

But these builders of the new world will have to be careful not to erect a new prison, be it an ideal and enlightened one. In fact, they will understand, and quickly, that this City of Truth will not and cannot see the light of day until they themselves live totally in the Truth, and that that building site is first and foremost the site of their own transmutation. One does not deceive Truth.

One may deceive men, make speeches and declarations of principle, but Truth doesn't care a damn. It catches you in the act and throws your deception right back into your face at every step. It is a merciless searchlight, even if it is invisible. And it is very simple; it catches you every time, at every twist and turn; and since it is a Truth of matter, it foils your plans, checks your gesture, confronts you with a sudden lack of materials, workers or funds, stirs up revolt, sets people at odds with each other, sows impossibilities and chaos – until, suddenly, the seeker realizes that he was on the wrong track, putting up the old false structure with new bricks and exuding his small egoism, small ambition or small ideal, his narrow idea of truth and good. So he opens his eyes, opens his hands, attunes himself again to the great Law, lets the rhythm flow, and becomes clear, clear and transparent, plastic to the Truth, to the something seeking to be – anything as long as it be *that*, the exact gesture, the right thought, the true work, the pure truth expressing itself as it wishes, when it wishes, in the way it wishes. For a second he lets go of everything. For a second he calls out to that new world – so new he understands nothing of it, but which he wants to serve, embody, grow in this rebellious soil. What does it matter what he thinks, feels or deems, oh, what difference does it really make? – just let it be the true thing, the one necessary and inevitable thing. And everything tips into the light – in a second. Everything instantly becomes possible: the materials arrive, and the workers and the funds, the wall crumbles, and the little egoistic structure he was building changes into a dynamic possibility he had not even suspected. He repeats this experience a hundred times, a thousand times, at every level, personal and collective, from the repair of his bedroom window to the sudden million that comes as a "godsend" to build that Olympic stadium.

There are no material problems, ever; there are only inner problems. And if Truth is not there, even the millions will rot on the spot. It is a fabulous experience every minute, a test of Truth and, even more marvelously, a test of the power of Truth. Step by step he learns to discover the effectiveness of Truth, the supreme effectiveness of a clear little second—he enters a world of continuous little marvels. He learns to trust Truth, as if all those blows, blunders, conflicts and confusion were leading him knowingly, patiently, but relentlessly to take the right attitude, to discover the true lever, the true look, the cry of truth that topples walls and makes every possibility blossom amid the impossible chaos. It is an accelerated transmutation, multiplied by the resistance of each one as much as by the goodwill of each one—as if, truly, both resistance and goodwill, good and evil, had to be changed into something else, another will, a will-vision of Truth that decides the gesture and action at each instant. This is the only law of the City of the Future, its only government: a clear vision that accords with the total Harmony, and spontaneously translates the perceived Truth into action. The fakers are automatically eliminated by the very pressure of the Force of Truth, driven out, like fish, by a sheer excess of oxygen. And if one day these ten or fifty could build a single little pyramid of truth, whose every stone has been laid with the right note, the right vibration, simple love, a clear look and a call to the future, the whole city would actually be built, because they would have built the being of the future in themselves. And perhaps the whole earth would find itself changed by it, because there is only one body, because the difficulty of the one is the difficulty of the world, the resistance and darkness of the other are the resistance and darkness of the whole world, and because that insignificant little enterprise of a tiny city under the stars may be the very Enterprise of the world, the symbol of its transmutation, the alchemy of its pain, the possibility of a new earth by the single transfiguration of one piece of earth and one piece of mankind.

It is therefore probable that for a long time this City under construction will be a place where negative possibilities will be exacerbated as much as the positive ones, under the relentless pressure of the beacon of Truth. And falsehood is skilled at holding on to insignificant details, resistance at sticking to everyday trifles, which become the very sign of refusal. Falsehood knows how to make great sacrifices. It can follow a discipline, extol an ideal, collect merit badges and Brownie points, but it betrays itself in the insignificant—that is its last refuge. It is really in matter that the game is played out. This City of the Future is a battlefield, a difficult adventure. What is decided over there with machine guns, guerilla warfare and glorious deeds is decided here with sordid details and an invisible warfare against falsehood. But a single victory won over petty human egoism is more pregnant with consequences for the earth than the rearranging of all the frontiers of Asia, for this frontier and this egoism are the original barbed wire that divides the world.

*
* *

For that matter, the apprentice superman could begin his battle very early, not just in himself but in his children, and not just from their birth but right from their conception.

We are born in a lead casing. It surrounds us completely. It is airtight and invisible, but it is there all the same, covering our least gestures and reactions. We are born "ready-made," as it were, but the making is not of our own, neither in the best nor in the worst. There are millions of sensations, which are not yet thoughts, but like seeds of desire or repulsion, odors of fear, odors of anguish, like a subtle fungus lining our caves: layers upon layers of prohibitions and taboos, and a few rare permissions thrown in like an escape of the same dark onrush in our tunnels. And, in the middle of all that, a bewildered and lost little look—who will soon be taught "life," good and evil, geometry and the Tables of the Law. A little look getting more and more veiled, and definitely lost after he has been made to understand everything. For the obvious and natural assumption is that a child understands nothing and has to be taught how to live. But it could be that a child understands very well, even if that does not agree with our constructs, and that we merely teach him to bury his knowledge and replace it with a ready-made science, which buries him for good. Then we spend thirty years of our life undoing what they have done, unless we are a particularly successful subject, that is, definitively immured, satisfied, polite and holding degrees. Hence, a great part of the work involves not "doing" but undoing that spell. We will be told that this struggle is fruitful, enriching, that it develops our muscles and personality—that is wrong. It hardens us, develops fighting muscles in us and may well drive us into an "against" as noxious as the "for." Moreover, it does not develop a personality, but a mask, for the true person is there, totally there, artless and wide open, in the eyes of a newborn child—we only add the misery of the struggle. We believe utterly, intensely and blindly in the power of suffering; it has been the subconscious mark of our entire Western civilization for the last two thousand years. Perhaps it was necessary, given the denseness of our substance. But the law of suffering is a law of Falsehood—what is true smiles, that's all. Suffering is a sign of falsehood, the product of falsehood; they go hand and hand. To believe that suffering is enriching is to believe that cancer is a boon from the gods, although cancer, too, can help us break the shell of falsehood. Like all virtues, this negative virtue leaves a permanent shadow on us; and even the unobscured sun is still blemished by it. The blows, truly and necessarily, leave their mark; they produce liberated beings with scorched hearts who remember having suffered. That memory is yet another veil over the artless look. The law of the gods is a sunlit one. And perhaps the whole work of Sri Aurobindo and Mother is to have brought the world the possibility of a sunlit path on which suffering, pain and disaster are no longer necessary in order to progress.

The apprentice superman does not believe in suffering. He believes in enrichment through joy; he believes in Harmony. He does not believe in education; he believes in the power of truth in the heart of all things and all beings—he only helps that truth to grow with as little interference as possible. He trusts in the powers of that truth. He knows that man always moves toward his goal, inexorably, despite everything he is told or taught—he only tries to suppress that "despite." He simply waters that little sapling of truth—and then again, with some caution, for some saplings prefer a sandy and rocky soil. But, at least, in that City—or rather, laboratory of the future—the child will be born in less stifling conditions. He will not be brainwashed, met at every street corner by screaming posters, corrupted by television or poisoned by vulgar movies, not burdened by all the vibrations of anxiety, fear or desire that his mother may have conscientiously accumulated in her womb through "entertaining" reading, debilitating films or a torn home life—for everything is recorded, the slightest vibration, the least shock; everything enters the embryo freely, remains and accumulates there. The Greeks knew this well, and the Egyptians and the Indians, who used to surround the mother with special conditions of beauty and harmony so that the breath of the gods could pervade each day and each breath of the child, so that everything could be an inspiration of truth. And when the mother and father decided to have a child, they did it as a prayer, a sacrifice for incarnating the gods of the future. It takes only a spark of aspiration, a flame of entreaty, a luminous breath in the mother's heart for the same light to answer and come down, the identical flame, the kindred intensity of life – if we are gray and dull, we will summon only the grayness and nothingness of millions of lifeless men.

The child of that City will be born with a flame, consciously, voluntarily, without having to undo millenia of animality or abysses of prejudice. He will not be told incessantly that he has to earn a living, for nobody will earn a living in the City of the Future, nobody will have money. Living will be devoted to serving the Truth, each according to his capacity or talent, and the only earnings will be joy. He will not be deluged with musts or mustnots; he will only be shown the immediate sadness of not listening to the right little note. He will not be tormented with the idea of finding a job, being a success, outranking others, passing or failing grades, for nobody succeeds or fails in the City of the Future, nobody has "a job," nobody takes precedence over anybody; one does the one job of pursuing a clear little note that lights up everything, does everything for one, takes care of everything for one, unites everything in its tranquil harmony, and whose only success is to be in accord with itself and with the whole. He will not learn to depend on a teacher, a book or a machine, but to rely on that little flame inside, that sprightly little flowing that guides his steps, prompts a discovery, leads by chance to an experience and brings out knowledge effortlessly. And he will learn to cultivate the powers of his body the way others today cultivate the powers of push buttons. His faculties will not be confined in ready-made forms of vision and comprehension; in him will be fostered a vision that has nothing to do with the eyes, a comprehension that is not from books, dreams of other worlds that prepare tomorrow's, direct communications and instant intuitions and subtle senses. And if machines are still used in the City of the Future, he will be told that they are temporary crutches until we find in our own heart the source of the pure Power which will one day transmute matter as we now transmute a blank sheet of paper into a green prairie with the stroke of a pencil. He will be taught the Look, the true and potent look, the look that creates, that changes everything – he will be taught to use his own powers and to believe in his power of truth, and that the purer and clearer he is, in harmony with the Law, the more matter responds to Truth. And, instead of entering a prison, the child will enter an open world where everything is possible – where everything is *actually* possible – for there is no impossibility except the one we believe in. Finally, the child will grow up in an atmosphere of natural oneness, free of "you," "me," "yours" or "mine," where he will not have been taught constantly to put up screens and mental barriers, but to be consciously what he unconsciously has been since the beginning of time: to extend himself into all that is and lives, to feel in all that feels, to comprehend through an identical more profound breathing, through a silence that carries everything, to recognize the same little flame everywhere, to love the same clear little flowing everywhere, and to be the self everywhere, behind a thousand different faces and in a thousand musics that are a single music.

Then there will be no more boundaries inside or outside, no more "I want," "I take," no more lack or absence, no more confined and lonely self, no more against or for, good or evil. There will be one single supreme Harmony in thousands of bodies, plucking its chord in this one and that one, this circumstance and that accident, this gesture and that one, unifying everything in one single movement whose every second is perfect and every act true, every word exact, every thought right, every line rhythmical, every heart in unison—and Truth will mold matter according to its right vision. And this little city without boundaries will radiate by its simple power of truth, attracting what must be attracted, discarding what must be discarded, simply by its own force of concentration, touching this point of the universe or that one, this soul or that one, answering thousands of invisible calls, continuously emitting its high, clear note which will brighten the world and lighten hearts, unbeknownst to all.

For such is Truth, so simple no one sees it, so light it travels around the world in a second, unties knots, crosses boundaries and pours out its marvelous possibility in the midst of all the impossibilities, at the slightest call.

13
And Then?

WE DO NOT have the power because we do not have total vision. If, by some miracle, power were given to us – any power, on any level – we would instantly turn it into a lovely prison corresponding to our small ideas and sense of good, we would lock our whole family up in it, and the world, if we could. But what do we know of the good of the world? What do we know even of our own good, we who today lament this misfortune only to realize tomorrow that it was knocking at the door of a greater good? For the last two thousand years and more, we have been devising beneficial systems, which crumble one after another – fortunately. Even the wise Plato banished poets from his *Republic*, much as today we would perhaps banish those useless eccentrics who roam the world and knock blindly at the doors of the future. We complain about our incapacity (to heal, help, cure, save), but it is exactly, minutely commensurate with our capacity of vision – and the philanthropists are far from being the most gifted. We are forever running up against the same mistake: we want to change the world without first changing ourselves.

The superman has lost his small self, lost his small

ideas of family and country, good and evil – he has in effect no more ideas, or has them all, exactly when needed. And when one comes, it is carried out, very simply, because its time and moment have come. For him, ideas and feelings are simply the imperative translation of a movement of force – a will-idea or force-idea – which is expressed here by this gesture, there by that action or plan, this poem, that architecture or cantata. But it is one and the same Force in different languages – pictorial, musical, material or economic. He is tuned in to the Rhythm, and he translates according to his particular talent and place in the whole. He is a translator of the Rhythm.

> *There every thought and feeling is an act,*
> *And every act a symbol and a sign,*
> *And every symbol hides a living power.* 31

But when nothing impels him, he is perfectly still and tranquil, like the lotus on the pond, drinking in the rays of the sun, without a quiver, without a ripple, without the least trace of "I want" anywhere – he only wants what *that* wants. And as for the rest, he is simply aglow in the sun, leaving it to others to gather a little honey (or not, for he shines for everyone). This is the simple state par excellence, the simplicity of the Truth. And the instantaneous effectiveness of the Truth without screens.

But his tranquil silence is not inactivity – nothing is inactive in the world, not "even the inertia of the clod, even the silence of the immobile Buddha on the verge of Nirvana." 32 He is distinguished from others neither by ecstatic meditations atop a festooned *gaddi* 33 nor by a white beard and immaculate clothing. He attends to the trifling details of life, and no one knows who he is. He cares nothing about being recognized, he who recognizes

all. And those trifling details are the minute lever with
which he operates on all similar substances throughout
the world, for there are no boundaries anywhere, except
in our heads and our small imprisoned body – life extends
infinitely, and this birdcall answers that birdcall, this sorrow, a thousand sorrows. His whole life is a meditation.

Its stillness bears the voices of the world[34]

His gestures are the symbol of a great Rite that embraces the stars and the movement of crowds, together
with this young locust sapling and that wayside encounter.

He may also lead a revolution or accomplish an awe-
inspiring and striking deed, if such is the flow of the
Truth in him. He is unpredictable, elusive as Truth itself;
he chaffs as he looks grave and smiles as he pores over
the world's misery; for he listens to invisible calls and
works ceaselessly to pour the Rhythm over the earth's
wounds. He does not perform miracles that flare up like a
flash in the pan, then leave the earth to its unrepentant
darkness; he does not play with occult *siddhis*[35] that
upset the laws of matter for a time, then let it fall back into its old routine of pain; he has no need to convert men
or preach to nations, for he knows all too well that men
are not converted by ideas or words or by sensational
demonstrations, but by a change of inner density, which
creates a sudden little breath of ease and sunshine in the
darkness – he sows another law in the world, opens the
window to another sun; he changes the density of hearts
by the tranquil outpouring of his ray. He does not strike
or break, does not condemn or judge; he tries to free the
same particle of truth contained in each being and each
thing and each event, and convert each by its *own* sun.
His power is a power of truth to truth, of matter to mat-

ter, and his vision embraces everything, because he has
found the little point within that contains all points and
beings and places. In this beggar walking by, that cloud
tinged with pink, this chance accident, the little nothing
that jostles his house or the young shoot growing, he sees
the whole earth and its millions of buds growing toward
their kindred Truth, and the world's exact position in a
faltering of chance or the remark of a passerby. Everything is his field of action. Through the minuscule, he
acts upon the whole; in the minuscule, he deciphers the
whole. From one end of the world to the other, he
touches his own body.

But the work is not finished. Evolution has not reached
its summit; it has not even entered its solar Truth. If the
Work were to stop here, we would have reached the summit of man and produced a super-man, but not the being
of the next age. Our widened consciousness, our direct
perceptions, our refined senses, our exact gestures and
movements, our perfect actions, our right thoughts and
right wills, our unalterable joy would still rest upon an
animal body—an aging, precarious and decaying body,
which would threaten our luminous poise with abrupt collapse at every moment, checking the operation of our
truth-consciousness with a tiny grain of sand—and what
kind of truth is that if it is so fragile? Truth is or is not,
and it is immortal, infinite, invulnerable. It is light and
luminous, incorruptible, and it cannot be prevented from
being all that it is, any more than the mango tree can prevent itself from being a full tree with all its flowers and
every one of its golden fruits. It will not stop at that
limited accomplishment and will not rest until the whole
earth and all beings are in its likeness, since the whole
earth and all beings are in fact its own seeds. The superman, too, is a "transitional being." He is the forerunner of
another being on earth, as different from man as we are

from the ape, and maybe even more, for man is still made
of the same substance as the ape while the new being will
be made of another substance – immortal, luminous and
light as Truth itself. He is the elaborator of the "supramental being" announced by Sri Aurobindo, and his substance is the humble laboratory of a perilous adventure.

Our body's cells must hold the Immortal's flame.
Else would the spirit reach alone its source
Leaving a half-saved world to its dubious fate. [36]

For the point is not to produce a mind endowed with
miraculous and luminous powers, to impose on this body
a law superior to its own, or even to push the physical
substance to its supreme degree of refinement, but "to
create a new physical nature,"[37] and yet out of this body,
this poor, frail animal body, since it is our very base, our
instrument of evolution. The new being will not come out
of the clear blue sky, ready-made. We have to make it!
We have to find the key to our own transmutation in our
substance, the Secret of all secrets in the microscopic, in
the smallest cell. It is in our body that the transition, the
difficult passage, must be effected. If we capture that
Secret, perhaps we shall have the divine key to matter,
the key to the long earthly pilgrimage, and the radiant
and potent look that one day launched us on our journey.
We must knock at the door of death and free its powerful
secret – for Truth hides there too, since everything that is
is Truth. We must unseal the rock of the Inconscient and
find the primal base, the solar foundation upon which all
existence rests. We have to touch rock bottom in order to
touch the supreme Sun. Within a cell of our body lies the
identical mystery of all galaxies and all earths. One point,
one miniscule point, contains all – the supreme Power
and ever radiant Truth, the supreme darkness and death

eternal (or so it seems), bound together in a perilous embrace pregnant with an inconceivable Possibility. Another mystery summons us.

> *A voice arose that was so sweet and terrible*
> *It thrilled the heart with love and pain, as if all hell*
> *Tuned with all heaven in one inextricable note.*
> *Born from abysmal depths on highest heights to float,*
> *It carried all sorrow that the souls of creatures share,*
> *Yet hinted every rapture that the gods can bear.* [38]

It is up to us to unravel this knot, this mortal mixture, up to us to find the key and dare the supreme adventure.

The path of descent is not yet finished.

14

The Victory Over Death

THE SEEKER has followed step by step the process of demechanization. Degree after degree, he has unraveled and cleared the various levels of entanglement that prevented the free flow of Harmony. He is no longer caught up in the mental machinery or the vital machinery; to a certain extent, he is no longer caught up in the subconscious machinery. The gray elf is still there, but like a shadow on a movie screen, a lingering memory of pain, a sort of old but still sensitive wound. It really no longer has any hold, except through that shadow, which taints joy and leaves a dull feeling of uneasiness in the depths, an unfathomable something still unhealed, a sort of lurking Threat without a face or a name—something is still there, like the memory of a catastrophe that can unleash catastrophe at any moment—as if everything were in fact terribly precarious and one forgetful second were enough to tip everything over into the old mortal habit again. There remains a point, a formidable point, and so long as that point has not been conquered, nothing is conquered, nothing is definitively certain. One does not quite know what triggers that sudden swing to the other side, the mortal and painful side, the old, anguish-laden and threatening side. (It is a state of threat, a threat in everything, the instantaneous mantle of lead, the old nameless and throat-constricting thing, as though in one second—one suffocating little second—millenia of night and suffering and shame came bursting into the setting and everything suddenly looked like a brilliant picture plastered on that black, untouched density, which sucks one into its destructive dizziness.) That dark swing sweeps down on you abruptly, without reason, strips you of all your suns, and leaves you naked, as at the beginning of time, before the old Enemy—perhaps the foremost enemy of man and life upon earth, an ineffable mystery that wraps you in its embrace, a dreadful vertical fall that is as if tinged with love and the great Fear. You do not know what provokes it—apparently no error, no slackening of tension, no wrong movement of consciousness that would reopen that forgotten dungeon—but it is wide open. And indeed something has been forgotten; and so long as that forgetting has not been unforgotten, the great golden Memory of Truth will be unable to shine its entire Sun over our entire being. And that Enemy, that shadow, is perhaps the disguised Lover who lures us into his supreme pursuit, his ultimate discovery. We are guided each step of the way. An infallible Hand outlines its meanders in order to take us directly, through a thousand detours, to its happy totality:

> *The one inevitable supreme result*
> *No will can take away and no doom change,*
> *The crown of conscious Immortality,*
> *The godhead promised to our struggling souls*
> *When first man's heart dared death and suffered life.* [39]

Hence, it is not through an arbitrary and morbid decision of his own that the seeker will undertake this dark descent – for a long time he has stopped willing anything, he only obeys the little rhythm, the flowing that is growing in him, and directs it here or there according to where it presses. The descent takes place gradually, almost unknown to him, but it is accompanied, as it were, by certain phenomena which become increasingly clear and define the "psychological conditions" of the descent. These psychological conditions are threefold. There is that little "flowing" we have often spoken about, there is that "rhythm," and there is that "fire" of being which opens the doors of the new world. One may be tempted to think that this is a poetic fiction, an imagery for children, but it is nothing of the sort, and the whole world is a poem becoming true, an image becoming clear, a rhythm taking body. Little by little, a Child looks at the world with eyes of Truth and discovers the lovely Image that was always there; he listens to an undying Rhythm and, attuned to that Rhythm, he enters the immortality he had never ceased to be. That flowing actually grows, that rhythm becomes clearer, that fire intensifies as the first mental and vital layers are clarified. In fact, it is no longer simply a "flowing" but a sort of continuous current, a descending mass that envelops first the crown of the head and the nape of the neck, then the chest, the heart, the solar plexus, the abdomen, the sex organs, the legs, and which even seems to reach under the feet, as if there were an extension of being all the way down there, an abyss of existence. The farther the current descends, the warmer and more compact and denser, almost solid, it becomes – it feels like an unmoving cataract. The descent is proportionate to our degree of clarification and the downthrust of the Force (which grows as we become clearer). No mental or psychoanalytical machinery has the power to reach those deeper layers. The movement is irresistibly powerful, sometimes even doubling one over, as if crushing one under the pressure. But at the same time as the power grows so does the stability, as if finally, at the end of the descent, there were a motionless mass of energy – or with such an intense vibration, so swift and instantaneous, that it seems solidified, immobile, yet moving unbelievably fast in place – a "powdering of warm gold," says Mother. This is what Sri Aurobindo called the supramental Force. It would almost seem as if it became "supramental," or acquired supramental qualities, as it descends into matter (that is to say, as we consent to let it go through, as the resistances fall away under its pressure and it victoriously penetrates all the way down to the bottom). We say "supramental," but it is the same with this word as with everything else: there is only one Force, as there is only one moon, which gradually becomes full to our vision, but the moon was always full and the Force always the same. It is our receptivity which changes and makes it look different from what it always was. It is that "flowing" which spontaneously, automatically, without any will or decision on our part (all our wills add more confusion), effects the descent, overturns obstacles, exposes falsehoods under its relentless searchlight, exposes the gray elf, brings to light all our hiding places, cleanses, purifies, widens and brings infinity to each level and into each cranny – and does not give up, does not stop for a second until everything, down to the least detail, the smallest movement, is restored to its original joy, its infinity, its light, its clear vision, its right will and divine acquiescence. This is the Force of the yoga, the Consciousness-Force Sri Aurobindo spoke of. It is the one which forges the superman, the one which will forge the supramental being – the one which will forge itself in that forgetfulness of itself.

Thy golden Light came down into my brain
And the grey rooms of mind sun-touched became
A bright reply to Wisdom's occult plane....
Thy golden Light came down into my throat,
And all my speech is now a tune divine....
My words are drunk with the Immortal's wine.
Thy golden Light came down into my heart
Smiting my life with thy eternity....
Thy golden Light came down into my feet:
My earth is now thy playfield and thy seat. [40]

Then there is that "fire." This is not a myth either: "The red-glowing mass of him is seen," says the Veda, "(*Agni*, the fire) adorable, great of body, wide of light." [41] At the beginning, however, this body is just a little spark, its red-glowing mass, a flickering flame sometimes lit but often extinguished, which has to be relit again and again. It is a tiny cry of suffocation in the world's night, a nameless need walking with us, going up and down our meanderings, following us tenaciously like a memory of something else, a golden recollection amid the grayness of the days, a call for air, a need for space, a need of loving, a need of being true. And this cry, this fire, grows:

Man is a narrow bridge, a call that grows. [42]

At first it is just a little flame in the mind, something groping about in search of a vaster inspiration, a greater truth, a purer knowledge, which soars, soars, and would as soon cut away all the weight of the world, the hindrances, the bonds and tangles of the earth. It soars and sometimes emerges, pure, sharp, upon summits of white light where everything is forever known and true – but the earth, meanwhile, remains false; life and body remain in the dark conflict, and die and decay. So this white little flame begins to take in the heart. It yearns to love, to heal, to save. It gropes about in the dark, helps a fellowman, gives assistance, offers itself and sings a song that would like to embrace all, contain all, take all life into its heart. It is already a warmer and denser flame, but its minutes of illumination are like a pale and fragile firefly on an ocean of obscure life. It is constantly quenched, engulfed, swept under the wave and under our own waves of obscurity—nothing is changed and life continues in its rut. So the seeker decides to drive this fire, this ardent truth, into his every moment and gesture, into his sleep and into his days, into his good and into his evil, into his whole life, so that everything may be purified, consumed by that fire—so that something *else* may be born at last, a truer life, a truer being. He enters upon the path of the superman. And the fire continues to grow. It goes down and down the degrees of the being, plunges into the subconscious caves, dislodges the gray elf, disloges the misery within, and burns more and more continuously, powerfully, as if stoked by the obscure pressure. It is already a body almost in our likeness, vermillion-red in color, already verging on gold. But it is still fluctuating and precarious; it lacks a fundamental base, a permanent foundation. So the seeker decides to drive this fire into his substance and body. He wants his own matter to reflect the Truth, to incarnate the Truth; he wants the outside to radiate as the inside. He enters upon the path of the supramental being. For, in truth, this growing self of fire, this ardent body which bears more and more resemblance to our divine archetype, our brother of light up above, and which seems to exceed us on all sides and even to radiate all around with an already orange vibration, is the very body that will form the supramental being. It is the next earthly substance, "harder than the diamond and yet more fluid than the gas," said Sri Aurobindo.[43] It is the spiritual condensation of the great Energy before it becomes matter.

But how to induce this fire into our matter, how to effect the passage, or transfusion, of this dark and mortal body to that ardent and immortal one? The work is in progress; it is difficult to talk about. We will not really know how it is done until it is done. No one knows the country or the way to it since no one has ever gone there. No one has ever made a supramental body! But it will be made, as inevitably as man and the ape and the millipede were already made in the great golden Seed of the world. This is the last adventure of the earth, or maybe the first of a more marvelous series on a new earth of truth. We do not know the secret; we only know in what direction to walk—though knowing the direction is perhaps already knowing the secret, since it unfolds under our steps and is formed by walking it.

So we can at least indicate the direction, the simple direction, for as usual the secrets are simple. *The fire is built by the particle of consciousness we put into an unconscious act.* Viewed from above, it is unconsciousness resisting and heating up from the friction of the new consciousness seeking entry—it is that futile and automatic gesture which has trouble untwisting its habitual groove and turning differently, under another impulsion; and we have to untwist the old turn a thousand times, insist and persist until a little flame of consciousness replaces the dark routine. Viewed from below, it is that unconsciousness which suffocates and calls out and knocks and seeks. And both are true. It is the memory within which summons the golden ray; it is the great eternal Sun which makes that call for sunlight well up. The process, the great Process, is simple: we must light that little fire by degrees, put the ray into each gesture, each movement, each breath, each body function. Instead of doing things as usual, automatically, mechanically, we must remember Truth there too, yearn for Truth there too, infuse Truth there too. And we meet with resistance, forgetfulness, breakdowns; the machine goes on strike, falls ill, refuses to take the path of light. We must begin again thousands and thousands of times, point by point, gesture by gesture, function by function. We must remember again and again. Then, all of a sudden, in one little point of the body, in that passing little breath, something no longer vibrates in the old way, no longer works as usual; our breathing suddenly follows another rhythm, becomes wide and sunny, like a comfortable lungful of air, a breath of an air never known before, never tasted before, which refreshes everything, cures everything, even nourishes as if we were inhaling the nectar of the immortals. Then everything falls back into the old habit. We must start all over again, on one point, on another point, at each instant — life becomes filled with an extreme preoccupation, an intense absorption. A second's minuscule victory strengthens us for another discovery, another victory. And we begin to work in every nook and cranny, every movement; we would like everything to be filled with truth and with that sun which changes everything, gives another flavor to everything, another rhythm, another plenitude. The body itself then begins to awaken, to yearn for truth, for sunshine. It begins to light its own fire of aspiration here and there, begins to want not to forget anymore; and whenever it forgets that new little vibration, it suddenly feels suffocated, as if it were sliding back into death. The process is simple, infinite, perpetual: each gesture or operation accomplished with a particle of consciousness binds that consciousness, that little fire of being, to the gesture or operation, and gradually transforms it. It is an infusion of consciousness, a microscopic and methodical and innumerable infusion of fire, until matter itself, under that conscious pressure, awakens to the need of consciousness as the seed awakens to the need for sunlight. Everything then starts growing together, inevitably, irresistibly, under that golden attraction. By degrees, the fire is lit, the vibration radiates, the note spreads, the cells respond to the Influx. The body inaugurates a new type of functioning, a functioning of conscious truth.

The body's virtue is its obstinate permanence; once it has learned something, it never forgets it—it goes on repeating its luminous functioning twenty-four hours a day, day and night, with the same obstinacy with which it used to repeat its diseases, fears, weaknesses and all its dark, age-old animal functioning.

This bodily "demechanization" therefore resembles that of the upper, mental and vital levels, but instead of filling a wasteland of mental unconsciousness between this lamppost and that one, from one end of the street to the other, we must fill a wasteland of bodily unconsciousness between this breathing and that one, this movement and that one, from one end of the body to the other. Instead of confronting a mental machinery churning out a thousand futile thoughts, we face a bodily machinery secreting a thousand imperceptible fears, apprehensions, morbid memories, and turning in a circle in its old, dark arteries. And each "recall," each interruption of the machinery to fix the look of consciousness upon this obscure process creates and binds its droplet of light, its brief moment of being, its little fire, adding one drop to another, and finally begins to make another flow in those veins, another rhythm and another song, and a new bodily ardor that feels like another body in the body, a sort of luminous double which becomes the support, the "driver," we could say, of the old shadowy body. It is this luminous double that will ultimately replace (?) or transmute the other. It is the next earthly body, the "Son of the body" the Vedic Rishis spoke of.

In short, we must replace the "program" automatically fed into the cells and the whole inexorable ribonucleic code that keeps secreting its little distress signals and glandular calls with a conscious "program," a call for light, a solar code in that rattle of valves and pistons and wandering enzymes which, while they make up for our weaknesses and plug the holes of our incapability to absorb directly the great current of restorative Harmony, lock us up in a dungeon of microscopic energy that is soon exhausted and decomposed.

A new spiritual training of the body has to be invented.

Like the other changes of program — mental, vital and subconscious — this change of bodily, cellular program is, as one can gather, extremely upsetting to the old equilibrium, for the very first task of Truth is always to sow chaos, that is, to dislodge falsehood, aim its searchlight and expose all the little rats burrowing in the recesses of the body, or the thousand and one bacteria of death, we should say. If wrong thoughts and wrong impulses are the falsehoods of the mind and heart, illnesses are the falsehoods of the body — and death the foremost of all falsehoods. But, as usual, our falsehoods turn out to be not so much a fundamental error or fundamental falseness as a resistance against a higher order. This resistance is life's protection — and its entombment. We always regard illness as a struggle against a noxious and destructive agent, but it may be, first, the superficial sign of a struggle against truth and a refusal of truth, which spontaneously and automatically invites death. The seeker will therefore be confronted by the falsehoods of the body; illness and death will become his daily battle-field, maybe even hour by hour and minute by minute – flash-illnesses and flash-deaths – in order for him to learn the trade of Truth and the immortal code in this mortality. But *death* is a word for something that does not exist. One does not die when one leaves one's body, any more than when one goes from one room to another or changes clothes. Actually, death is not "on the other side"; it is right here, at every instant, inextricably mingled with life; we take it along everywhere we go and, sometimes, it *becomes* death. That "sometimes," that moment, or more complete movement of death in us, is what we must catch hold of. Death is not "another state," an accident suddenly thrusting us into something else. It is ingrained in life itself; it is its base, its dark foundation. And if we could unravel those tightly knit threads, that death in the quick, that self of death that beats softly within us and tries day after day, almost hour after hour and every instant, to sup-plant our self of truth, we would have the key to prolong-ing life at will. One dies only from want of truth. It is the only want in the world. If we were totally true, we would be totally immortal. Death is dissolution of falsehood – for falsehood is in essence decay – and we will die only so long as we are not truthful from head to toe and in every cell of our body. In short, death is the keeper of Truth, the dark angel standing at the immortal threshold that destroys anything incapable of passing purely into Truth. We have already crossed the threshold in our purified mind; we have perhaps crossed it in our heart and feelings – we must cross it in our body. The self of truth must completely replace the self of death. The process of immortalization takes place from the top down: first in the mind, then in the heart and senses, then in the body – but the supreme resistance is also the supreme victory.

It is indeed a resistance. Death is a resistance to the law of Truth, to the ever-renewed flow of Harmony. Deep down, we are founded on the "rock of the Inconscient"[44] the Vedic Rishis spoke of, the rock that is perhaps the first moment when the great Energy solidified, turned into matter, plunged into a dark contradiction of itself, "sank" into an inert stillness of its triumphant flow, lost itself in a black, motionless ecstasy that was like the inversion of its solar ecstasy on the summits. Those who have had the experience of descending into the material Inconscient know that the image of the Vedic Rishis is not just an image but a rather formidable reality to go through. It is truly a rock – immense and seemingly bottomless – a sheer drop into a basalt chasm, which cannot even be termed black because there is not one spark of blackness there, not one glimmer that would permit one to call it black – it is *the* Blackness, absolute, without one breath, without one vibration of anything whatever: an instantaneous suffocation, a mortal stifling, a world utterly still, utterly closed, as if strangled on itself, without a sound, without a movement, without an echo of anything whatsoever. An utter void, and yet like a black, asphyxiating existence, something that *is* in spite of everything – but is like a density of absolute negation, a tremendous refusal which raises its walls of basalt and plunges, plunges like an abyss into an abyss, like a death into a death. To descend there is in fact like dying. It is death. It is the Inconscient. One *cannot* be there; one *must not* be there. It is like a supreme repudiation of everything that moves and breathes, everything that bears a particle of light making it possible to live. It does not move. It does not breathe. It is a NO. A tremendous NO to everything and of everything, which swallows you or expels you – or forces you to summon a light greater than that Darkness.

And there is only one light greater than that thick, stifling Blackness: the supreme Light, the Great Sun of Truth.

This is why it is said in the Upanishads that Yama, the god of death, is the son of the Sun.[45]

The supreme sun is at the bottom of the supreme darkness. "Death" is the passage to immortality, the keeper of the great total Sun, the ultimate compulsion toward integral Truth. At that moment, whatever is incapable of summoning the Light, all the unpurified fragments of being are immediately snapped up by that NO, dissolved in it, frozen in its black ecstasy, because they are themselves a little spark of that NO, a little refusal of that great Refusal, a chip of that formidable Rock.

And, as a result, we have the key to everything that creates death in life – our countless little deaths every minute. And we understand that this body, this ever so fragile and insignificant little body, which others reject as an old rag or a hindrance to the supreme frolicking of the liberated Spirit, is in fact the site of a supreme conquest and a supreme deliverance, and that the heaven of the Sun of Truth is carved out on earth and in our body every minute by our adherence to or refusal of the light, by our choice, minute by minute, between our self of light and our self of death.

The supramental being is one forever delivered from death and, through his deliverance, the earth will be delivered, compelled to her supreme Sun by her supreme darkness.

15

The Transformed Being

THE SEEKER of the integral truth is therefore like a battler of death, but that was in fact what he had been doing
all along, ever since he stopped a minute on that
boulevard to pierce that dark rush of the machine with
his cry. He has struggled against the falsehood of unconsciousness in his mind, in his heart, in his life and every
gesture, and in his subconscious; and now falsehood
shows its real face: It was death that paraded about the
boulevards of the mind, in the recesses of the heart and
the caves of the gray elf, death that secretly invited the
corrosive thoughts, the dark slippages of desire, the grip
of the ego. Behind that unrelenting quest of thirst and
possession, behind the thousand questions of the mind,
the thousand craving gestures, there were as if two mortal arms yearning to interlock forever and press against a
heart, quiet at last, the great satiety of a nothing without
desire, without a breath, without the least tension of pain
anywhere. The gray elf has assumed its face of stone; the
mental ego has laid the last brick of its impregnable
fortress. Our brilliant masteries are the masteries of
death; one day, they let the cat out of the bag, when the
imprisonment is complete: the dead man inside comes

to superimpose himself on the dead man outside, exactly,
as we have built him gesture by gesture. One does not
go to the other side; one always has been on the side of
death. But for the battler of Truth, the game becomes
clear. Ten times, a hundred times a day he catches
himself going to the side of death; he crosses the line
again and again, tilts imperceptibly into falsehood with
minute nothings in which death takes refuge, goes back
and forth between life and death in his body's arteries.
He learns the technique of the passage. He sorts out the
mortal mixture.

> *I left the surface gods of mind*
> *And life's unsatisfied seas*
> *And plunged through the body's alleys blind*
> *To the nether mysteries.* [46]

It is a long, monumental work. Each victory changes
into defeat; each defeat becomes a greater victory; and it
must be begun again at another point, and still another,
endlessly. And we seem to hear Sri Aurobindo's moving
voice at the end of the long journey, his cry of indomi-
table certitude reverberating through the fragile walls of
death:

> *I made an assignation with the Night; ...*
> *And traveled through a vastness dim and blind*
> *To the grey shore where her ignorant waters roll.*
> *I walk by the chill wave through the dull slime*
> *And still that weary journeying knows no end;*
> *Lost is the lustrous godhead beyond Time,*
> *There comes no voice of the celestial Friend,*
> *And yet I know my footprints' track shall be*
> *A pathway towards Immortality.* [47]

But this is still a negative way of saying things, for the traveler of the sunlit path seeks neither hells nor Night, nor the tiny flash-deaths, though they sometimes befall him in a cry of suffocation. He seeks to remain always tuned in to the great flow of Harmony and Light and Truth, in everything he does, his every function, every breath of air he takes, every heartbeat. He is a meticulous colonizer of the Light. He pushes it into every nook and cranny of his body, into his sleep as well as his waking, into every activity, every movement, every dark alley of the body, as in the past on the boulevards outside, and he gains ground step by step, cell by cell. He lights the fire of need – need for truth, need for light, need for space – in every one of those infinitesimal fortresses and pushes back ever farther the line of unconsciousness. Illnesses befall him, his strength declines,* death smirks for an instant, but this is no longer even a trap or a fall, for he has his eyes wide open and sees that an infallible Hand has led him into this abyss so he can light a fire of truth there, too, a cry for help, a need of space and infinity – and the second the true cry bursts out, everything vanishes; illness, death, all are gone in a split second, like an unreal dream. He learns the unreality of death. It is the supreme unreality; it crumbles in the twinkling of an eye under a single little breath of truth. But if we believe in it, it is instantaneous death. The implacable flow of basalt swallows us up into its nothingness – which is

---

* Indeed he is far more conscious of the old vital forces he is losing than of the new forces he is acquiring, which are subtler, unusual for his body, and whose workings he is not familiar with – they seem to vanish in one second, by a minute shift of consciousness, and to return also in one second and refresh him, by another shift of consciousness which he does not fully understand yet. But that one little second of refreshment is inexpressibly more invigorating than hours of physical rest and seems to put everything back in order from top to bottom, like a complete renewal of the being.

nothing really, nonexistent; the cry of a child pierces it effortlessly! There is but one reality, which is the immortal Truth, the eternal Sun, the great and soft flowing that moves the worlds and bodies—if we want to believe in it, want to let ourselves be carried by It; if we consent to the sunlit path. It is the only Reality. Death does not exist; it is only the forgetting of *That*. A second of recall, and everything sparkles in the sun again—everything has never ceased sparkling in the sun. There was never any shadow, never any death; there was that false look. Death is a false look. The world is growing toward its true Look, which will change everything into what it really is; it is growing toward its Fire, which will transmute everything into what it really is. The Truth of one point will unveil the Truth of all points; the Truth of matter will act on every fragment of matter—and death and the shadow and the NO buried in the heart of the world will reveal their immortal face, their eternal light, their consenting and glorious YES, because they will have touched their supreme bottom and completed their mission, which was to take us to the gates of the Sun, in our body and upon an earth of truth.

But tracking down falsehood and unconsciousness in the body would still not bring us immortality. It would only prolong life at will. And "who would care to wear one coat for a hundred years or be confined in one narrow and changeless lodging unto a long eternity," said Sri Aurobindo. [48] To perpetuate life in its present coarse functioning would indeed be a dreadful burden, which we would soon wish to be rid of. Thus, this prolongation of life at will is only a first operational step to give us the time to build the supramental being in our body. Doing it takes time; it is a race between the swiftness of death and the speed of the transformation. Sri Aurobindo estimated that it would take three hundred years to form that being. But it does seem that the movement is accelerating more and more, and perhaps that supreme transformation does not depend so much on the length of time of individual preparation as it does on the preparation of the earth body as a whole and on its ability to accept the new world. And the Force of the New World is pounding the earth mercilessly; it is advancing with giant strides. The seams are cracking, and what seemed like a distant peal is becoming a thunderous death knell, which hides the next resurrection. We are touching rock bottom; we are before the gate of the deep Night which veils the unexpected.

All's miracle here and can by miracle change. [49]

* *

This genesis of the supramental being is not really a distinct stage; it is intimately mingled with that of the superman, and only the mind forces us to draw partitioning lines. Actually, it is a long journey through lives and ages, body after body, the slow growth of a little fire within, no bigger than a firefly, which was already hidden in the atom, the stone, the plant, and which has become conscious of itself in man, which has grown through struggle and pain, experience after experience in a brown skin or a white one, under this latitude or another, which has emerged in the mind as a cold ray, split the darkness into a thousand contradictory beams, which has beat in the heart like a warm little flame, struggled and striven against wind and tide, toiled in love and toiled in grief and toiled in pleasure; which has pierced this shell of life, shone for nothing, pure, like an autumn bonfire on the shores of the world, searched here and searched there, kindled its flame with a thousand nothings that never made plenitude, set the days and hours ablaze, taken in the minutes, the big gestures and the small, the cold seasons and the hot, until there was a single season of fire, a single song of flame here and there. And it has become the body of our body, the heart of our heart, the high thought springing from the white flamings of the Spirit, the pure vision piercing the pain of appearances, the pure love like a vermillion snow upon the sad fields of the earth, the pure music, the pure rhythm attuned to everything—it has become our body of prayer for the world, our body of light for mankind, our ardent body for the earth's future, our living pyre for matter's transfiguration. And the deeper it plunged into that dense darkness, that negation in the depths, that pettiness of a thousand gestures and heartbeats for nothing and routines of death, the brighter it became, the more it shone, the more golden it glowed like a sun, became concrete, as if it were on the verge of an ultimate transfusion, a golden invasion of matter, one last cry of love that would topple the walls and bring forth the living glory of the new body, of the Master of all this evolution. "O Fire . . . the flaming rays of thy might rush abroad on every side violently," says the Veda. "The Flame with a hundred treasures . . . O Son of the body . . . Thou foundest the mortal in a supreme immortality."[50]

One day he will emerge, the Master of the long journey of fire, the goal of all those sufferings, the epitome of the ages. And the whole earth will be changed by it, seized by its irresistible ray of joy and beauty, won over to the smile by a smile. And all the shadows will be dispelled, as though they had never existed.

One man's perfection still can save the world.[51]

His Look of truth will unveil the true look in each of us. His pure Truth will make the same Truth shine in every heart and every atom. His Reality will make the world real. The earth will be transfigured by the irresistible radiance of her own Sun.

Only joy can convert to joy.

*
* *

What will that supramental body be like, that "life divine" on earth? Here again, miracles will turn out to be the simple nature of the world and the new life to follow a divine logic, the logic of the divine truth of matter. What will be is already here, crude, coarse, scarcely aware of itself, limited by our own limited vision, for truly the world is a vision being unveiled. That stupendous, innumerable, inexhaustible Energy, that Consciousness-Force, that immense Harmony we are cut from—barricaded as we are in an egoistic little body, confined in a little quiver of desire and pain—will flow through us unimpeded, because our self will have become the world's self, our mind the transmitter of the great rhythm, our heart the diffuser of the great throbbing of oneness, our law the one sunlit Law that moves the worlds, and our body the symbol of the great earthly body. There will be no more false note in us, no more personal screen, no more distorting glass, no more egoistic will, but the one Will that moves the worlds and the one note that makes the spheres sing. The Harmony will then be able to flow at all the levels of our body, directly, mightily, purely. The little centers of consciousness,[52] the chakras of the various plexuses, will have become powerful condensers of the cosmic Energy, its projectors onto matter. They will nourish our own body directly the way today food nourishes us indirectly and heavily. They will each receive the exact vibration corresponding to their function, the light "frequency" corresponding to their action: the rays of the instant will-thought that executes, the flashes of the truth-vision that puts things into place and opens up and frees the truth of each being, each object, each circumstance, the sun of the heart that heals, the flood of Life-Force that sweeps away obstacles, the great ray of the original Force that fashions matter by the truth of matter. All the nerves, tissues, cells that we have demechanized, purified, freed from their congestion of unconsciousness will become free channels for the supramental Force and will flood our body with the lights of the Spirit, with the Joy of the Spirit, with the immortal nectar — until the day this golden Influx is sufficiently concentrated and individualized to replace the heavy functioning of the organs and shows through all the pores of the old skin, permeating and transmuting the gross body, or reabsorbing it into its solar blaze, as the powerful gravitation of atoms reabsorbs the particles and frees their body of radiant energy.

We know nothing, nothing at all of the ultimate movement! But it will take place, as unavoidably as the laburnum pod bursts open to release its golden cascade. The mortal body will have finished its work, which was to generate an immortal body on earth by its own cry and to reveal the Spirit forever contained in its dark cells.

The freed supramental being will then be able to move within his own fluid, light, luminous solar substance, to travel at will, to withdraw into an invisible self-concentration or project himself victoriously outside, to change color and shape according to his state of being, level of concentration or operational need, to communicate directly and musically, to handle matter at will, modify it at will, recreate or reshape it at will, by the simple and direct manipulation of the vibration of truth in things, to build at will, dissolve at will and perform simply and instantly all the operations that our machines accomplish indirectly through a clumsy translation of our mental powers. For, in truth, he is a "supramental" being not because he is endowed with a super-mind poised one degree higher than the mind and possessing a more imperative power over matter, but because he is endowed with a more interior degree of power, which does not impose itself on matter or wrest violent miracles from it, but releases its own creative energy, its own creative joy, and makes it sing its own note of light the way the shepherd makes his pipe sing.

And life outside will obey life inside.

It will be the end of the Artifice. This fabulous, monstrous world bristling with machines on every floor and every level—swallowed up by a machinery that swallows us and swallows life's slightest movement, the least breath of thought, the lightest heartbeat, that rolls us under its enormous armored tank in which those richest in false powers, most armed with deceptive words, most affluent in false colors and tinsel and fake, artificial television lights, whose shell of triumphant unconsciousness is the heaviest, dominate a hypnotized mass which consents to this barbarous sacrifice to Moloch, this universal and total slavery, detailed down to the tiniest subconscious reaction, in which even the most enlightened men are still impelled by the muffled reverberation of the Machine, alienated from their own powers of seeing, feeling and communicating, smothered beneath an enormous apparatus that conditions their thought and feelings and beliefs, regimented by science, regimented by the law, regimented by the Machine one must keep clicking in order to live, eat, breathe and travel, keep alive in order to stay alive—will vanish like some unreal nightmare under the tranquil gaze of Truth,

which will put each thing in its place, endow the truer
ones with power, clothe each according to his own light,
illuminate each one in his true color, expose the innermost vibration without subterfuge, without false
clothing, rank beings spontaneously, automatically,
visibly, according to the quality of their flame and the intensity of their joy, impart its powerful rhythm to the
clearer ones, give to each a world in his measure, a dwelling in his color, an immortal body attuned to his joy, a
scope of action commensurate with the scope of his own
ray, a power to mold and use matter proportionate to his
intensity of truth, his capacity for beauty and his degree
of genuine imagination. For, in the end, Truth is Beauty,
is supreme Imagination which, through those millions of
years and billions of sorrows, sought to make us
rediscover our own power of loving, of creating and of
uprooting death through immortal joy.

But how will this matter, as heavy and stubborn as it is,
this unfeeling rock, obey the power of the Spirit? How
will the earth's matter allow itself to be transformed
without being crushed, violated, pulverized by some
sledgehammer of one kind or another, heated to a few
thousand degrees in our nuclear kettles? We might as
well ask how that rock could ever escape the tortuous
climb of the caterpillar—we see no farther than our mental conditioning, but our vision is false and the matter we
crush without mercy is as living, active, responsive as the
stream of stars above our heads or the invisible quivering
of the lotus under the summer sun. Matter too is living; it
too is a substance of the Eternal, and it can respond as
much as the mind, heart or plant. Only we have to find
the point of contact, to know the true language, just as
we have found the language of numbers, only to extract a
few monsters. Another language needs to be found for
another vision, a concrete language that imparts the

experience of what it names, brings to light what it says, touches what it expresses, which does not translate but materializes the vibrations and moves things by emitting the same note. A whole magic of the Word needs to be found again.

For there is also a Rhythm, which is not a fiction either, any more than that "fire" or "flowing" is. They are one and the same thing with a triple face,* in its individual and universal aspects, in its human condensation or interstellar space, in this rock or that bird. Each thing, each being has its rhythm, as well as each event and the return of the birds from the north. It is the world's great Rite, its indivisible symphony from which we are separated in a little mental body. But that rhythm is there, in the heart of everything and in spite of everything, for without it everything would disintegrate and be scattered. It is the prime bonding agent, the musical network that ties things together, their innermost vibration, the color of their soul and their note. The ancient Tantric texts said, "The Natural Name of anything is the sound which is produced by the action of the moving forces that constitute it."[53] It is the real Name of each thing, its power of being, and our real and unique name among the billions of appearances. It is what we are and what *is* behind all the vocabularies and pseudonyms that science and law inflict upon us and upon the world. And perhaps this whole quest of the world, this tormented evolution, this struggle of things and beings, is a slow quest for its real name, its singular identity, its true music under this enormous parody—we are no longer anybody! We are anyone at all in the mental hubbub that passes from one to another; and yet, we are a unique note, a little note which struggles

---

* Does not the *Rig-Veda* say, in one of its striking phrases, "This is he [the flame] who has the word of the truth." (I.59.7)

toward its greater music, which rasps and grates and suffers because it cannot be sung. We are an irreplaceable person behind this carnival of false names; we are a Name that is our unique tonality, our little beacon of being, our simple consecration in the great Consecration of the world, and yet which connects us secretly to all other beacons and all other names. To know that Name is to know all names. To name a thing is to be able to recreate it by its music, to seize the similar forces in their harmonic network. The supramental being is first and foremost the "knower of the Word" the Vedic Rishis spoke of, "the priest of the Word,"[54] "the one who does" by simply invoking the truth of things, *poïetēs* – he is the Poet of the future age. And his poem is an outpouring of truth whose every fact-creating and matter-creating syllable is attuned to the Great Harmony: a re-creation of matter through the music of truth in matter. He is the Poet of Matter. Through this music, he transmutes; through this music, he communicates; through this music, he knows and loves – because, in truth, that Rhythm is the very vibration of the Love that conceived the worlds and carries them forever in its song.

We have forgotten that little note, the simple note that fills hearts and fills everything, as if the world were suddenly bemisted in orange tenderness, vast and profound as a fathomless love, so old, so old it seems to embrace the ages, to well up from the depths of time, from the depths of sorrow, all the sorrows of the earth and all its nights, its wanderings, its millions of painful paths life after life, its millions of departed faces, its extinct and annihilated loves, which suddenly come back to seize us again amid that orange explosion – as if we had been all those pains and faces and beings on the millions of paths of the earth, and all their songs of hope and despair, all their lost and departed loves, all their never-extinguished music—in that one little golden note which bursts out for a second on the wild foam and fills everything with an indescribable orange communion, a total comprehension, a music of triumphant sweetness behind the pain and chaos, an overflowing instantaneousness, as if we were in the Goal forever.

We have reached the shore.

The supramental being and the superman are only the perfection of that little note. They are there! They are coming! They are knocking at the door of our age:

I saw them cross the twilight of an age,
The sun-eyed children of a marvelous dawn, . . .
The massive barrier-breakers of the world, . . .
The architects of immortality. . . .
Bodies made beautiful by the Spirit's light,
Carrying the magic word, the mystic fire,
Carrying the Dionysian cup of joy. [55]

And they will topple our walls.

16

The Season of Truth

THERE still remains the irritating secret of the transition between that body of light and this body of darkness, that body of truth and this mortal body. We have spoken of "transfusion" or perhaps reabsorption of one into the other, and also of transmutation of one by the other. But these are words that hide our ignorance. How will this "husk," as She who continued Sri Aurobindo's work used to call it (and who dared the perilous adventure, the last great saltus of material evolution), be opened, give way to that long-nurtured flower of fire? How will that new material substance – the substance of the new world – make its appearance, materialize? For it is already there; it will not fall from the sky. It is already radiating for those who have the truth-vision. It has been built, condensed, by the flame of aspiration of a few bodies. It almost seems as if a mere nothing would be enough to bring it out into the open, visible and tangible to all – but we do not know what that "nothing" is, that impalpable veil, that ultimate screen, or what will make it fall. It is nothing, really, scarcely a husk, and behind, throbbing and vibrating, is the new world, so intense, radiant and warm, with such a swift rhythm and vivid light, so much more vivid and true than the earth's present light that one really wonders how living in this old callous, narrow, thick and awkward substance is still possible, and that the entire life as it is does seem like an old dried-up husk, thin and flat and colorless, a sort of caricature of the real life, a two-dimensional image of another *material* world full of depths and vibrancy, of superimposed and fused meanings, of real life, real joy, real movement. Here, outside, there are only little puppets of being moving about, passing figures in a shadow dance, lit up by something else, cast by something else, which is the life of their shadow, the light of their night, the sacred meaning of their futile little gesture, the real body of their pale silhouette. And yet, it is a *material* world, absolutely material, not some glorious fiction, not a hallucination with eyes closed, not a vague aura of little saints. It is *there*. It is like "real matter," Sri Aurobindo used to say. It is knocking at our doors, seeking to exist for our eyes and in our bodies, hammering away at the world, as if the great eternal Image were trying to enter the small one, the true world to enter this caricature which is coming to grief on all sides, the Truth of matter to enter this false and illusory coating — as though the illusion were actually on this side, in this false look at matter, this false mental structure which prevents us from seeing things *as they are*. For they already *are*, as the fullness of the moon already is, only hidden to our shadow vision.

This solidity of the shadow, this effectiveness of the illusion, is probably the little "nothing" that stands in the way. Could the caterpillar have prevented itself from seeing a linear world, so concrete and objective for it, so incomplete and subjective for us? Our earth is not complete; our life is not complete; our matter itself is not complete. It is knocking, knocking to become one and full. It could well be that the whole falsehood of the earth lies in its false look, which results in a false life, a false action, a false being that *is not*, that cries out to be, that knocks and knocks on our doors and on the doors of the world. And yet, this "husk" does exist—it suffers, it dies. It is not an illusion, even if, behind, lies the light of its shadow, the source of its gesture, the real face of its mask. What prevents the connection? . . . Perhaps simply something in the old substance that still takes itself for its shadow instead of taking itself for its sun—perhaps is it only a matter of a conversion of our material consciousness, of its total and integral change-over from the small shadow to the great Person? A changeover which is like a death, a swing into such a radical otherness that it amounts to a disintegration of the old fellow. An instantaneous death-resurrection? A sudden other view, a plunge into Life—true life—which abolishes or "unrealizes" the old shadow?

The whole course, the simple course, is perhaps only to notice what is already there—and to learn to trust.

But this unyielding husk, this old illusory matter everywhere under our feet, continues to exist, at least for others. Its prevailing perception is the criterion of objectivity, what we call the world as it is. Is it conceivable that a handful of more advanced beings, of pioneers of the new world, will live in that true way, that true body (invisible to others), while others will continue living and seeing in the old shadow, stumbling along and suffering and dying with it, until they too become capable of effecting the ultimate conversion and entering the new world—which will become the prevailing objectivity—yet on this earth and in this matter, but seen with the true look? The old husk would fall off when everyone is capable of seeing with the same look—when everyone, thrust into a more advanced "season," would see the tree in bloom rather than the old pod? . . . The tree is in bloom because the season has come. Perhaps we must wait till men realize that the season has come and that all the flowers are there, on the beautiful tree—they are indeed there, except for those who dawdle in winter when spring is breaking out all over. The supramental consciousness, the supramental rhythm, is actually an extraordinarily swift rhythm—the present earth seems immobile and stagnant compared to that rhythm—and maybe that simple "acceleration" is what makes all the difference, what brings out the orange sweetness of the supramental radiation, its warm and vivid depths, its light earth, the way the acceleration of the galaxies turns the stars red or purple depending on their direction. How could this new vision, as concrete as that of all the Himalayas put together, even more concrete because it discloses all the innermost depths of the Himalayas and their living peace, their solid eternity, not radically change the whole life of humanity, at least for those who can see, and gradually for everybody, as radically as man's perception changed the world as perceived by the caterpillar? . . . For, ultimately, this new vision does not abolish the world; it reveals it *as it is* (and this supramental "as it is" is also capable of growing with future ages—where is the end?). It is not true that matter suddenly becomes "different" by some miraculous and transmuting stroke—it becomes (for our eyes) what it always was. It ceases to be this winding and steep caterpillar trail to level out into its sun-drenched prairies, which extend farther and farther with our look. True matter, supramental matter, was forever awaiting our true look—only like recognizes like. The divine season is waiting for us on earth, if we consent to recognize this Like of which we are now only a semblance. And the whole problem of the transmutation arises again: Is it a transmutation of matter or a transmutation of vision? Doubtless it is both, but the change of vision is what triggers the change of matter; the change in vision is what permits a new manipulation of matter, as our human eyes have enabled a new manipulation of the world. And this change of matter seems possible only if humanity as a whole, or a sufficiently effective proportion of the great earthly body – because we are a single body, we always forget – consents to breathe the new air, to soak up that sap, to stop believing in its phantoms and fears and old mental impossibilities. And we can believe – we can even *see* that this change of vision is contagious. There is contagion of Truth, an irrepressible spreading of Truth. It is Truth that is breaking our molds and our human consciousnesses and our law and our systems and our countries under its invisible golden pressure – the world is under a solar spell, which is shaking our age and throwing it into panic by its influx of vigor, and the Truth of a few will force all the rest to change, as simply and inevitably as the first touch of spring spreads from branch to branch and bursts out from bud to bud.

The secrets are simple, we have said, and we wonder if that "difficult" transmutation, that complex alchemy, those thick manuals and mysterious initiations, those educated austerities and spiritual exercises, those meditations and retreats and tortured breathing, that whole labor of the spirit are not actually the labor of the mind trying to make it difficult, tremendously difficult, so it can inflate itself further, and then glory in untying the enormous knot it had itself tied. If things are too simple, it does not believe in them, because it has nothing to do – because it *yearns* to do, at all costs. That is its food and livelihood – its ego's livelihood. But that mental inflation and pontification may hide from us an utter simplicity, a supreme facility, a supreme nondoing that is the art of doing all. We have had to do and do again, tramp around the trails of the mind to individualize a fragment of that formidable, immense Consciousness-Force, that universal Energy-Harmony, to make it self-conscious, as it were, in one form and in billions of forms. But has not the time come, at the end of the little flame's long journey, to break the mold that helped us to grow and rediscover the totality of Consciousness and Energy and Harmony in one small center of being, a little point of matter, in one clear little note, and to let *That* do, *That* change our eyes, *That* permeate our tissues, *That* widen our substance—to let a supreme Child who runs over the great prairies of the world play in us, a Child who asks nothing better than to play with us and for us, if we want, because he is us? This difficult transmutation may not be so difficult after all. It must be as simple as truth, simple as a smile, simple as a child at play. Perhaps everything hinges simply on whether we wish to take the path of difficulty—the path of the mind desperately inflating itself to try to blow itself up to the size of the universe, the path of the "buts" and "whys" and "hows" and all the implacable laws that choke us time and again in our mental straitjacket—or the path of an unknown little something stealing through the air, sparkling in the air, winking at every street corner and every encounter, in everything, all the trifles of the day, as though carrying us along in an indescribable golden wake in which everything is easy and simple and miraculous—we are right in the midst of the miracle! We are in the full supramental season. It is knocking at all our closed windows, at our countries, our hearts, our crumbling systems, our shaky laws, our faltering wisdoms, in our thousands of ills that keep coming out, our thousands of little lies abandoning the skiff in distress—it is softly slipping its golden skiff beneath the old specious appearances, it is growing its unexpected buds beneath the old rags, awaiting a tiny little crack to spring out into the open, a tiny little call. The transmutation is not difficult; it is all there, already done, only waiting for us to open our eyes to the unreality of misery and falsehood and death and our impotence—to the unreality of the mind and the laws of the mind. It is waiting for our radical saltus into that future of truth, our mass uprising against the old cage, our general strike against the Machine. Oh! let us leave it to the elders, the old elders of the old world, the old believers in misery and suffering and the bomb and the gospel and the millions of gospels that struggle for a share of the world, to run their old squeaky machine for a few more days, to quarrel over borders, argue over reforms of the rot, debate agreements of disagreement, stockpile bombs and false knowledge and libraries and museums, preach good and evil, preach the friend and the enemy, preach country and no-country, build more and more machines and supermachines and rockets to the moon and misery for every pocketbook—let us leave to them the last convulsions of the falsehood, the last cries of the rot, we who do not care about countries, borders, machines and all that walled-in future, we who believe in a light and inexpressible something that is pounding at the doors of the world and pounding in our hearts, in a completely new future, completely clear and vibrant and marvelous, without borders, without laws, without gospels, beyond all their possibilities and impossibilities, their good and evil, their small countries and small thoughts—we who believe in Truth, in the supreme beauty of Truth, the supreme joy of Truth, the supreme power of Truth. We are the sons of a more marvelous Future which is already there, which will spring out into the open by our cry of trust, sweeping away all the old machinery like an unreal dream, a nightmare of the mind, an old windbag filled with only as much air as we still consent to lend it. The transmutation has to be done in our hearts, the last revolution to be carried out, the supramental revolution of the human species—as others had launched the human revolution among the apes—its great rebellion against the Machine, its general strike against mental knowledge, mental power and mental fabrications—against the mental prison—its mass defection from the old groove of pain, and its calling out for what has to be, its simple cry for truth amidst the rubble of the mental age: the truth, the truth, the truth, and nothing but the truth.

Then Truth shall be.

Because it is simple as a child and responds to the least call.

And it will do all for us.

References & Notes

Most quotations from Sri Aurobindo refer to the complete edition of his works in 30 volumes (the Centenary Edition) and are indicated by the volume number followed by the page. Reference is made in particular to the following volumes:

5 – *Collected Poems*
15 – *The Ideal of Human Unity*
17 – *The Hour of God*
20 – *The Synthesis of Yoga*
26 – *On Himself*
28 – *Savitri*
29 – *Savitri*

1. *Savitri*, 28:256.
2. Sri Aurobindo, *Savitri*, 28:370.
3. Sri Aurobindo, *The Hour of God*, 17:1.
4. *The Synthesis of Yoga*, 20:82.
5. Sri Aurobindo, "Musa Spiritus," 5:589.
6. Sri Aurobindo, "Journey's End," 5:570.
7. This ascending path has been described in *By the Body of the Earth* and the higher planes of the mind have been discussed in *Sri Aurobindo or the Adventure of Consciousness*.
8. Sri Aurobindo, "A God's Labour," 5:99.
9. *Rig Veda*, III.22.2.
10. *Rig Veda*, I.70.2.
11. *Rig Veda*, I.59.1.
12. *Rig Veda*, III.39.5
13. *Katha Upanishad*, V.8.

14. *Rig Veda*, II.1.12.
15. *Rig Veda*, I.179.1.
16. *Brihadaranyaka Upanishad*, IV.5.4.
17. *Thoughts and Aphorisms*, no. 383.
18. *Mundaka Up·nishad*, II.2.12.
19. *Swetaswatara Upanishad*, IV.3.4.
20. *C·handogya Upanishad*, VI.8.7.
21. *Rig Veda*, II.24.4.
22. A geometrical design used by Tantric occultists to materialize certain forces.
23. *Rig-Veda*, III.7.II.
24. Sri Aurobindo, "The Life Heavens," 5:575.
25. Sri Aurobindo, *The Ideal of Human Unity*, 15:558.
26. Nirodbaran, *Correspondence with Sri Aurobindo*, II.112.
27. Sri Aurobindo, "A God's Labour," 5:99.
28. Mother, *Conversation* of September 16, 1953.
29. Mother, *Some Words of the Mother*, p. 31.
30. Sri Aurobindo, *On Himself*, 26:375-76.
31. Sri Aurobindo, *Savitri*, 28:183.
32. Sri Aurobindo, *The Synthesis of Yoga*, 20:253.
33. Throne (in particular for spiritual leaders).
34. Sri Aurobindo, *Savitri*, 29:573.
35. Powers.
36. Sri Aurobindo, *Savitri*, 28:35.
37. Sri Aurobindo, *On Himself*, p.172.
38. Sri Aurobindo, "A Voice Arose," 5:117.
39. Sri Aurobindo, *Savitri*, 28:59.
40. Sri Aurobindo, "The Golden Light," 5:134.
41. *Rig-Veda*, V.1.2, V.1.9.
42. Sri Aurobindo, "The Dumb Inconscient," 5:163.
43. A.B. Purani, *Evening Talks with Sri Aurobindo*, II. 291.
44. *Rig-Veda*, I.71.2.
45. *Katha Upanishad*, I.I.7.
46. Sri Aurobindo, "A God's Labour," 5:101.
47. Sri Aurobindo, "The Pilgrim of the Night," 5:132.
48. *Thoughts and Aphorisms*, no. 376.
49. Sri Aurobindo, *Savitri*, 28:85.
50. *Rig-Veda*, I.97.5, I.59.7, III.4.2, I.31.7.
51. Sri Aurobindo, *Savitri*, 29:531.
52. See *Sri Aurobindo or the Adventure of Consciousness*.
53. Arthur Avalon, *The Serpent Power*, p.96.
54. *Rig-Veda*, I.10.1.
55. Sri Aurobindo, *Savitri*, 28:343-44.

Acknowledgments

We wish to extend our gratitude and sincere appreciation to The Foundation for World Education, which has made the printing of this book possible. The Foundation was created by the late Mrs. Eleanor Montgomery, who was a friend and a devotee of the Mother.

Our sincere thanks also to Eric Hughes, whose careful and professional proofreading of the manuscript and his love of the work have given the English polish this book deserves.